A
WALK *With Your*
FATHER

A 90 Day Devotional Journey

M. P. Erickson

WESTBOW
P R E S S®
A DIVISION OF THOMAS NELSON
& ZONDERVAN

WestBow Press books may be ordered through booksellers or by contacting:

WestBow Press
A Division of Thomas Nelson & Zondervan
1663 Liberty Drive
Bloomington, IN 47403
www.westbowpress.com
844-714-3454

Scripture quotation marked (NKJV) is taken from the New King James Version. Copyright © 1982 by Thomas Nelson, Inc. Used by permission. All rights reserved.

Scriptures marked (NLT) are taken from the Holy Bible, New Living Translation, copyright © 1996, 2004, 2015 by Tyndale House Foundation. Used by permission of Tyndale House Publishers Inc., Carol Stream, Illinois 60188. All rights reserved.

Scripture quotations marked (NASB) are taken from the NEW AMERICAN STANDARD BIBLE®, Copyright © 1960, 1962, 1963, 1968, 1971, 1972, 1973, 1975, 1977, 1995, 2020 by The Lockman Foundation. Used by permission.

ISBN: 979-8-3850-1555-9 (sc)
ISBN: 979-8-3850-1554-2 (e)

Print information available on the last page.

WestBow Press rev. date: 02/15/2024

"The apostles returned to Jesus from their ministry tour and told him all they had done and taught. Then Jesus said, 'Let's go off by ourselves to a quiet place and rest awhile.' He said this because there were so many people coming and going that Jesus and his apostles didn't even have time to eat. So they left by boat for a quiet place, where they could be alone."

— Mark 6:30-32, NLT

Often the best hikes are deep in the forest, far beyond the noise of the roads and crowds. I'm always amazed at how quiet those trails are. So quiet that you can hear your heartbeat and sometimes almost hear your own thoughts.

There is a reason Jesus made a habit of finding isolated places to rest, pray, and spend time with His Father. Away from the distractions there is a clarity you can't get when life gets noisy. It's a place of mind where all the dust has a chance to settle, and quality time can be spent.

Our culture seems at war with this peaceful time. Productivity and the sense of *doing something*, anything, so you can get ahead in life grasps its claws on your time. Until you free yourself from the grip of anxious productivity, it will be difficult for you to reach your fullest potential. And more importantly, it will be difficult for you to have that special, devoted place of meeting with your Father.

The good news is you don't have to wander deep in the wilderness for days to spend time with Him. You can meet with your Father anywhere. But only if you are willing to tune down the noise, even for a short while, and tune to the frequency of Heaven.

———

Take some time to evaluate in what ways you can trade distractions for solitude. Noise can come in many forms, including schedules, people, entertainment, or screen-time. Taking a break from unnecessary distractions is a great way to clear the common and make room for the sacred. Your Father is always wanting to spend time with you. And He can speak through the noise at times. But there is nothing quite like getting away, wherever that is, and making a place of solitude with Him.

Notes:

_____

_____

_____

_____

_____

*"And whatever you do, do it heartily, as to the Lord and
not to men, knowing that from the Lord you will receive the
reward of the inheritance; for you serve the Lord Christ."*

— Colossians 3:23-24, NKJV

Have you ever been stuck trying to figure out if you are more like Mary or more like Martha? Feeling that if you get too hung up on the details you wouldn't be able to just sit at His feet? Do yourself a favor and take a huge step back from those mental gymnastics.

What God is calling us to is a wholehearted devotion in every area of our life. To have our mind and heart so centered that everything we do is an act of worship to Him. Basically, we are to have Mary-like focus with even the Marth-like details. Because Martha's problem wasn't serving. It was becoming distracted from the Person she was serving.

The key is to use your service as an act of worship. That every small act you do for someone else is done as if you are serving Jesus Himself in that moment, because you really are.

No one can do it all. But out of the abundance of love God has shown us, and the gifting He has placed in us, we often can do more than we think we can. To serve in simple ways. To do even the smallest and simplest of tasks out of a love for the One who gave you the ability to do those things in the first place.

When you serve others like that, they get more than just some of their needs met. They get to see the love of Jesus in bodily form. They get to see the love that drives people to willingly serve when others won't. And they get to see the heart of the Father reaching out from His kids who choose to serve.

Ask yourself if you have lost your love for service towards others. Take inventory of your motivation, or lack of, for service. If you are going through the motions and have lost sight of the mission of love Jesus has called you to, then take the time to refocus. Ask God to fill your heart fresh today with His love. Ask Him to captivate you once again so you can look at others with His eyes and serve others with His heart.

Notes:

_____

_____

_____

_____

_____

"My brethren, count it all joy when you fall into various trials, knowing that the testing of your faith produces patience. But let patience have its perfect work, that you may be perfect and complete, lacking nothing."

— James 1:2-4, NKJV

Have hard times ever driven you to God? And after you went through hard times, what came out of you? Did you let the process shape you?

Desperation causes even the most jaded to reach out for help. When life approaches a boiling point, the temptation is to run or compromise and excuse it as a necessary action. But certain difficulties can't be avoided; and when you face them with the virtues God is working into you, what is in you flavors the situation like a steeping tea.

The testing of your faith produces patience; but patience shouldn't be the final product. After patience is formed, we must let patience produce something.

Patience is not inactivity. Instead, patience is incredibly proactive. Farmers are highly patient, and yet are also some of the busiest, hardest working people. They choose patience because they have faith in what is coming: harvest time. But they also realize they have a part to play in the process.

Their patience, in turn, produces something. It produces a hearty work ethic of planting, watering, and fertilizing their crops. It produces wise choices in future planning and prioritizing of time and resources. It produces trust that even though they do not see it now, they know they will later.

But what if life gets tough, is God still good? Is He still your Provider when you lose your job? Is He still your Healer when you get sick? Are His ways still best even when you are ridiculed for holding on to them?

When you are faced with trials, get excited. Because if you hold onto your patient trust in Him through it, God can then work His perfection into you.

———————

Take some time to allow God to show you the areas of your life He wants you to grow in. What He shows you may seem impossible, so ask Him to help you see things from His eyes. It's a partnership with God that will produce growth.

Notes:

_____

_____

_____

_____

_____

*"I will praise You, O Lord, with my whole heart;
I will tell of all Your marvelous works."*

– Psalm 9:1, NKJV

Have you ever talked to someone and felt you were only *half there*? Or doing a task and your heart really wasn't in it? Sometimes we can pinpoint the reason for our mixed feelings. But sometimes the answer is buried.

Do you find your prayers and times with your Father are a similar way? Is your mind and heart distracted with questions, worries, or doubts? Or are we too busy or tired to give our all when spending time with our Father? And if this is you, are you content? Or do you want something more?

The first step to living whole-heartedly towards you Father is to bring your whole heart to Him. Even the ugly parts. And yes, your doubts also. If you recognize a *block* between you and your Father confront it head on. If something is bubbling under the surface, bring it to your Father. Don't ignore or hide it. Clear the air. Ask the hard questions. If you know what it is, name it. If you don't, ask God to reveal it to you.

We must realize the power of our will. I often don't feel like praying or reading my bible, or almost any other Christian discipline. But the key is in the name: discipline. If I don't feel like spending time with my Father but want to be close to Him, I must engage my will and do those things I don't feel like doing. And yes, sometimes you must push through those *not feeling it* times to get to where you want to be. But when you develop healthy habits, you will often feel best when you continue in them.

It amazes me that our Father listens to us. We all know fathers are supposed to listen to their kids; but sometimes we lose the connection that God is a Father. All powerful, and yet He walks with us where we are at. Fills the universe, and yet takes the time to intentionally meet one-on-one with us. All knowing, and yet takes the time to listen to us even if we ramble a bit. We may not always get what we want. Or even feel the way we want. But we are heard and loved by a Father who is the best and truest example of what a father should be like.

Take some time to bring your whole heart, the good, bad, and ugly parts, and engage with your Father. Identify whatever issue or blockage there might be and expose it to His light. He knows best and can see far beyond what we can. He gave us His all but wants to give more. He knows what we can understand and wants to pull back the curtain and reveal more. All He is asking for is our whole heart.

Notes:

_____

_____

_____

_____

_____

"But sanctify the Lord God in your hearts, and always be ready to give a defense to everyone who asks you a reason for the hope that is in you, with meekness and fear."

– 1 Peter 3:15, NKJV

Are you ready to respond to the questions of others? Not to be defensive. Not to argue. But to give a reason and defense. Peter shows us how we should respond to the questions of others. Both those who are curious because they see our lifestyle and those who wish to slander or persecute you for your faith.

But you must first set Jesus as the most important and special person in your heart. When you sanctify Him in your heart, you root your confidence in Him instead of the questions or threats of others. The questions won't sway you. The fear of ridicule won't sway you. Even threats of harm can't steal what has been rooted as special in your heart.

It is like when others ask you what is most important to you. Those things that are special to you and bring a smile to your face when you talk about them. You know why they are important to you and what you would do for them. That knowledge is key because you know how to respond to others with what is close to your heart.

Do your actions show that Jesus is set apart, or sanctified, in your heart? Does your time show this truth? What would your answer be when confronted by the question: "Why do you have so much hope?"

How we communicate our reason is as important as what we say. We want to have wisdom to answer in a way that brings life (Proverbs 15:1-2) with meekness and fear. Or you could also say with gentleness and respect.

What is your reason for having hope no matter what life throws at you? Can you articulate it? Are you ready to explain at any time to anyone? Does it overflow from the special place you have given to God? If you can't, I have good news: you can change that now! But first things first. True life can only overflow from a heart filled with Jesus.

———

Take some time to evaluate if Jesus is truly set apart in your heart. Once He is, then you can form your answer. Once you can lay out why you have hope, practice it over and over so you are ready (2 Timothy 4:2).

Notes:

_____

_____

_____

_____

_____

"Then the Lord said to Joshua, 'This day I have rolled away the reproach of Egypt from you.' Therefore the name of the place is called Gilgal to this day."

— Joshua 5:9, NKJV (see also verses 1-12)

Do you carry shame from your past life? Or live under the shadow of your family history? Does it hang over you like a dark cloud threatening to rain guilt on the *new leaf* of your life? Do questions of doubt fill your mind making you feel like an imposter?

The adult children of the Israelites who doubted God were forced to walk in the desert for 40 years alongside their parents who had failed. Imagine the stigma they must have carried with them into the Promised Land. They had some successes in battle with Moses, and God did dry up the Jordan for them to cross. But when they had become adults, they were probably worried, wondering if they would mess up and be just like their parents.

But God did something powerful. He had Joshua circumcise all the men who were born or were children in the desert. Circumcision was a sign of the covenant God had with Israel and was a symbol of removing excess from our hearts and lives and exposing our hearts to God. God showed them He wasn't just the God of their parents, but He was their God also, and they didn't have to make the same mistakes.

Our Father wants to remove shame and guilt from our lives as well. But first we must allow Him to become not just the God of our parents, but *our* God. Any area not surrendered and exposed to the light of Jesus might never be fully healed.

What *excess* areas do you have in your life? What areas in your heart is God not allowed to heal? Is your heart hard towards Him? If you find any area in your life like this, it's time to circumcise your heart (Deuteronomy 10:16).

When the Israelites had healed and walked into their promise, they ate off the land for the first time and the manna they had been eating stopped. This weaning process of maturity is crucial to growing spiritually. But before we can go deeper with Him, we must heal from the past.

Take time to identify areas in your life that need healing. Once identified, stop hiding them and instead expose them to Jesus. Healing may come soon or may be a process. This almost always includes other believers, pastors, or counselors walking with you as you allow your Father to guide your steps. Choose wisely, and prayerfully consider people of integrity and character to go with you. And choose to begin walking in freedom.

Notes:

"Many are the afflictions of the righteous, but the Lord delivers him out of them all."

— Psalm 34:19, NKJV

I get mixed feelings while standing at the trailhead of a long climb. I know at some point my muscles will start aching and my backpack straps will dig into my shoulders. My knee and ankle joints will get sore. I might slip up, or get hurt, and my body will beg me to quit most of the way up. I know all this at the start and yet I still climb. So why would I willingly take a path that will lead me through hard stuff? Because I know what waits at the top, and the journey is well worth the price.

Every climber should be aware of what they will face before they begin. The same is true in life. We don't often want to focus on the bad stuff in life, and generally we shouldn't. But we also shouldn't be unaware of it either. Living a godly life as a Christian can keep us from many troubles if we listen to godly counsel. But also, if you choose to be a Christ follower on the path back to your Father, you will face trouble (2 Timothy 3:12).

Although it can take a great deal of discipline to live out the Christian disciplines, the real test comes when you face obstacles and opposition. What do you do when you have an uphill battle with no end in sight? How do you choose to react when you are scrutinized? You will be tested. You will be tried. You will face those who are opposed to you and everything you stand for when you side with your Father. You may even be persecuted and face loss.

We shouldn't have any doubt that following your Big Brother's footsteps back to our Father will be difficult. But it is rewarding (Hebrews 11:6). Sometimes God delivers us from hardships, and sometimes through them. Sometimes He keeps bad things from happening; and sometimes His strength is what gets us to the other side of difficulties. But the real reward is not what does or doesn't happen to us, but what we get both now and in the end.

Why should we live out this life as a Christian knowing we will face persecution? Because following Christ is the only way back to the Father (John 14:6). To be adopted back into our Father's family as sons and daughters. Our reward is eternal salvation from a horrible end that we justly deserved. And the end of taking this path is to be with Him forever.

Take some time to remember why you follow Christ. And if you haven't been faithful, take some time to renew your commitment to living as a child of your Father. Like any good father, He stands ready to take you back and walk with you. You might not see all the way to the end now, but you can't beat the view from the top!

Notes:

_____

_____

_____

_____

_____

"When He had come down from the mountain, great multitudes followed Him. And behold, a leper came and worshiped Him, saying, 'Lord, if You are willing, You can make me clean.' Then Jesus put out His hand and touched him, saying, 'I am willing; be cleansed.' Immediately his leprosy was cleansed. And Jesus said to him, 'See that you tell no one; but go your way, show yourself to the priest, and offer the gift that Moses commanded, as a testimony to them.'"

– Matthew 8:1-4, NKJV

Have you ever wondered why Jesus didn't want the former leper to tell everyone He had healed the man? Why did Jesus sometimes want them to keep it to themselves?

Leprosy was an awful life sentence many in that time dealt with. It was lonely, isolating, and constantly reminded you that you could never be a part of a community again.

But this man was different. He didn't resign himself to waste away as he was. Instead, he got desperate and chose to go against the law and approach the one who he knew could heal him. He was supposed to call out his condition by yelling "unclean". Instead, he chose to call out to the one who could make him clean.

Jesus didn't turn away from him. Instead, he did what no one else *would* do. He reached out and touched him. This might have been the first human touch this man had felt for a long time. Then after doing what no one else *would* do, Jesus did what no one else *could* do: healed him of his leprosy.

After giving the gift of His attention, His touch, and His healing power, He points the man back to His Father by telling him to offer his gift to the priest so he could be restored back into community as a living witness to everyone that God can still heal. Jesus took the time not only to restore him physically, but also relationally. Not just to his community, but also with a Father who loved him.

Take some time and ask God how you can show kindness to those you are around in a way that points them back to their Father. Take inventory of your gifts and talents and find ways of using them to point others to the Father who wants them back.

Notes:

_____

_____

_____

_____

_____

"Then Joshua said to the children of Israel: 'How long will you neglect to go and possess the land which the Lord God of your fathers has given you?'"

– Joshua 18:3, NKJV

Beware when laziness is cleverly disguised as patience. Beware when neglect of duty is excused as seeking God's guidance. Joshua's corrective words offer us a chance to look inward. Not to guilt ourselves, but to examine our efforts and hearts (Galatians 6:4, Psalm 26:2).

Each of us has been given gifts, talents, responsibilities, and callings. Created to be an influence in areas looking for an influencer. Yet instead of rising to the challenge, many get hung up in the endless trap of self-discovery and ignore the needs in front of them. Some sit and wait to be called instead of seeing all the areas God in His Word has already called us.

Did you know you are already called and have action plans you can operate in now? Did you know it's God's will that you go through the process of sanctification (1 Thes. 4:3-5)? Or to give your Father thanks in every situation (1 Thes. 5:18). Or to silence criticism by your good works (1 Peter 2:15).

We must also be able to hear from our Father ourselves. And that can be hard to do until we rid ourselves of our past mindsets. A mind being transformed will be able to prove what God's will is. But if we look too much like the systems of this world instead of the Kingdom God is trying to get on earth, it will be hard for us to identify God's perfect will for us (Romans 12:2).

What kind of people do you feel drawn to? What type of activity or ministry grips your heart? What abilities has God already given you? How many gifts can you, or others around you, identify in your life?

Take time to ask your Father to show you in His word what ways you have already been called. Spend time today building closeness in your relationship with your Father and ask Him what area in your heart He wants to deal with next.

Notes:

_____

_____

_____

_____

_____

"I wait for the Lord, my soul waits, and in His word I do hope. My soul waits for the Lord more than those who watch for the morning - yes, more than those who watch for the morning."

— Psalm 130:5-6, NKJV

Have you ever waited by the phone in anticipation of a call from a special someone? Or waited by the mailbox for an important delivery? Or counted down the days on a calendar until a special day finally arrived? In those instances, there is an anticipation and expectancy, rooted in hope, that drives us on. A deep knowing of the certainty of what is to come, like a child before Christmas.

Why don't we walk each day with that same, child-like anticipation that at any moment God could speak to us? And more than that, even wants to! Better to live your life saying, 'I don't know when or where, but I know He's going to speak to me soon!' What would the outcome be if we lived each day with that belief? Would God be more likely to speak to someone who carries this attitude, or one that says, 'God never talks to me!'

Doesn't every good father want to speak to his children? I know the Father wants to speak to me, just like I know the Father wants to speak to you. Even if I don't hear Him when or how I want, I know He will speak to me. Because of this, I make room for Him to speak when He is ready. And if you leave the *ears of your spirit* open, watching and waiting, you will be ready to listen.

Not only does He want you to listen with anticipation, but He also wants to hear from you. Wouldn't any good father also make room for his kids to speak? When you speak to God, believe that He will hear you (Hebrews 4:16). If sin is blocking your communication, confess it and ask for forgiveness. Your Father is ready to forgive if you are ready to ask for it.

Take some time to communicate with your Father. Spend time telling Him all the ways He is awesome. Confess sin. Admit fear. Leave nothing hidden. Then ask your Father to speak to you and, with anticipation, leave some empty room for Him to speak. It may not be when or how you want it but keep that door open. Cultivate the anticipation like His words are wrapped Christmas presents to us, and we His kids are anxiously waiting for Christmas morning!

Notes:

_____

_____

_____

_____

_____

"And behold, two blind men sitting by the road, when they heard that Jesus was passing by, cried out, saying, 'Have mercy on us, O Lord, Son of David!' Then the multitude warned them that they should be quiet; but they cried out all the more, saying, 'Have mercy on us, O Lord, Son of David!'"

— Matthew 20:30-31, NKJV

Are you willing to put aside your pride and be public with your reliance on your Father? Are you desperate enough for your Father to show up that you don't care who sees you expose your need for Him?

The two blind men had heard about Jesus and what He could do. When they heard He was near they seized their chance and wouldn't let go. Their desperation caused quite the scene. Those around them tried to shut them up, seeing only the embarrassment and inconvenience instead of seeing with the eyes of the Father.

But when you are desperate, shame and embarrassment do not have a hold on you. You abandon yourself until you get to the source. When you are desperate for what is real, only the true Source will do. You become willing to be specific and admit your problems, needs, and faults.

There is something beautiful that happens when we realize how desperately we need our Father. We often don't realize how deeply we need Him in every area of life until desperation drives us to cry out to Him. Then we get a small glimpse of our total need for Him.

How foolish the crowds must have felt when Jesus took the time to show compassion. If we hide our reliance on Him, then our Father's provision will likely also be hidden from the view of others. Not every situation is the same; some situations require more discretion. But in most cases when we get desperate and place confidence in our Father's leadership, others can be blessed when they see that there is a Father who can come through for them.

Take some time to examine any area you may be lacking desperation in. Do you believe that God is your provider, healer, leader, etc.? Do you hide your need for Him in front of others? Your desperation can also be a witness to those who need to return to their Father. Because when you get desperate and put your reliance in Him, then others can see a testimony of a Father who keeps His promises.

Notes:

_____

_____

_____

_____

_____

"Remember, the fire must be kept burning on the altar at all times. It must never go out."

– Leviticus 6:13 NLT

I sat at my campsite next to the fire I had worked so hard to build. It was hot enough that all I had to do was feed it a small stick every few minutes to keep it going. I knew if I left it alone for a while it would slowly die down and I would have to go through the whole process again to build it back up. But if I gave the fire the attention it needed, it would continue to thrive.

Some see the fire on the altar as a symbol of intimacy with God. But to me, the fire on the altar represents the readiness to humble ourselves and be rid of any excess or wrong we may be carrying. And once the fire burns away the old, the intimacy of a restored relationship can grow. But if we lose the soft tenderness of heart to admit fault and live transparent before our Father, then hardness of heart begins to set in as our *altar* cools.

Kindling the fire requires more than admitting fault. It means admitting our heart is out of alignment with His. The willfulness of doing our own thing and living our own way must burn away. Wrong patterns of thinking must burn away. Every attitude of the heart that doesn't conform with His heart for others must burn away. And if there isn't already an altar of readiness then one must be built up.

Thankfully we don't have to offer sacrifices of animals anymore to be forgiven; Jesus became our sacrifice. And if we come to Him asking forgiveness from our heart, we will have it. But every relationship must be kept up to date and fostered. And once Jesus saves you, He begins the work of saving you. He begins taking you on a long journey to mold and shape you. And to move forward with Him we must be willing to sacrifice what He points out.

Take some time to foster a fire of readiness with your Father. If you haven't already, it may take some time to build up that readiness to lay things down. But once built, just like a fire, it will be far easier to keep going. And when your Father points out areas needing change, take that as a sacrifice to the alter and lay it on the fire you have built one stick at a time.

Notes:

_____

_____

_____

_____

_____

"Don't copy the behavior and customs of this world, but let God transform you into a new person by changing the way you think. Then you will learn to know God's will for you, which is good and pleasing and perfect."

— Romans 12:2, NLT

"We do this by keeping our eyes on Jesus, the champion who initiates and perfects our faith."

— Hebrews 12:2a, NLT

Some things go unnoticed until we train our eyes to recognize them. And once we become familiar with it, we see it all the time. This happens to me a lot when I am building with my kid's building blocks. I'll paw through a bin looking for a certain piece, getting increasingly frustrated when I can't find it. But once I find that piece, I have a better picture in my mind of what it looks like and I begin to find more of them.

What you focus on more you will see more. The opposite is also true. The less you focus on something the less you will see it. This is true in most areas of life. From seeing reclusive animals on the trail to replaying old hurts in your mind. We decide every day what we want to focus on.

But when we focus on spiritual things it goes a step further. What we focus on we not only notice more, but we also become more like. We can grow towards the light or wither in the darkness. At times it can be hard to know what to focus on. But our Father didn't leave us without an example to follow. Knowing our imperfections, He sent His perfect Son for us to focus on and follow.

The ways of our Father are not the ways of the world we live in. When we first come to Him, we often bring our old mindsets, and then wonder why we are not seeing a change. But the change we seek may evade us until we allow our Father to change our minds. This can be hard at first, like trying to find something we have never looked for in the past. But if we fix our eyes on the ways of our Father, and put them into practice, His ways will become more familiar. And more importantly, His change can be worked in us.

Take some time to go over what you have been focusing on. Is what you have been allowing yourself to focus on from the heart of God, or from a heart broken by sin? Has your behavior looked more like a changed mind, or a mind that follows the systems of this world? Ask your Father what areas He wants to change today. When He points out an area needing change, focus on the example of Jesus in that area until that area looks more like Him.

Notes:

_____

_____

_____

_____

_____

"But you, be strong and do not let your hands be weak, for your work shall be rewarded!"

— 2 Chronicles 15:7, NKJV

"But without faith it is impossible to please Him, for he who comes to God must believe that He is, and that He is a rewarder of those who diligently seek Him."

— Hebrews 11:6, NKJV

My favorite mountain view is the view from the top. When I am rewarded by the views of distant peaks and valleys from above, I almost forget what it took to get there. But the only way to enjoy the view from the top is to climb the mountain. And when you push through, you are rewarded!

Do you pursue time with your Father even when you don't *feel* anything? Or make a place for Him at the table in your life? For most people it can be hard to act when you don't see instant results. Or to believe your Father will provide for your needs when provision hasn't come yet. But for those who follow where God leads, even though they can't see beyond one step ahead, there is a reward!

If your time with your Father isn't the same as before, don't lose heart. Speak to your soul and remind yourself of the truth: that God is a rewarder of those who keep pushing after Him, even when He seems hard to find in the dense forest of life. Don't listen to your deceptive heart! It will lie and tell you He isn't there when you don't feel Him. And don't rely on your brain; it will make excuses about why you should have felt Him or seen something happen by now.

We must have something more to stand on than our limited knowledge and fluctuating heart. What we need is the promise of the One who has never lied. The feelings of the One whose heart has always been after you. And the intellect of the One who knows all.

Take some time to intentionally pursue your Father. Ask yourself if you have believed any lies from your heart or head when things haven't gone the way you expected. Take those lies and those feelings and tell them to kick rocks! Instead, replace them with the truth of what God is speaking over you from His Word. He's never given up or stopped pursuing you. Make the choice to pursue Him with your whole heart and watch how He rewards you with His presence.

Notes:

_____

_____

_____

_____

_____

"Always be joyful. Never stop praying. Be thankful in all circumstances, for this is God's will for you who belong to Christ Jesus."

— 1 Thessalonians 5:16-18, NLT

After a long hike up to the peak I like taking time to look around at the views. It can be breathtaking with the hills, valleys, and snow-dusted trees for miles around. It always causes me to think about how big our God is. To be thankful that, despite being exhausted from the climb, I got to enjoy one small piece of His creation. Even though I knew I may never see that place again because tomorrow isn't guaranteed.

Do you find yourself more often being thankful, or unthankful? It's easy to be thankful when times are good. But the *tea-test* of what is deep in our hearts can only happen when we find ourselves in hot water. Difficult times show who you really are and what is in your heart.

But why should we be thankful for hard times? Why should we thank God when bad things happen? We shouldn't be thankful *for* everything, like sickness and death; but we should be thankful *in* everything. We might not be thankful for losing a job; but we can be thankful for an opportunity to rely on God's promises in our desperation. We may not be glad when we are criticized and mocked for holding to God's ways and standards; but we can be thankful in those times when character is formed in us.

A thankful heart is focused on the source of good instead of the cause of the problem. It's a perspective shift; not just to see the good, but to recognize and give credit to where every good thing comes from. It's more than the glass is half full. It recognizes whatever good is in that glass is from above. And if it is empty, trusts the promises of the One who can fill it!

Too many people wander about, asking what God's will is for them. After seeing the complexity of creation, it is tempting to think God's will for us must also be complex. Or maybe it is far simpler than we thought. That in every situation we find ourselves in, we should carry within us the joy that comes from Him. To communicate with Him on a regular basis. And no matter what we go through, to be thankful to our Father.

———————

Take some time to think of everything you can be thankful for. Be creative. Things that happened, that could have happened, or bad that was kept from happening. Are you healthy? Do you have food? Clothes? Focus all that thanks towards your Father. Because either directly or indirectly, all good things come from Him.

Notes:

_____

_____

_____

_____

_____

"James, a bondservant of God and of the Lord Jesus Christ, to the twelve tribes which are scattered abroad: Greetings. My brethren, count it all joy when you fall into various trials, knowing that the testing of your faith produces patience. But let patience have its perfect work, that you may be perfect and complete, lacking nothing."

– James 1:1-4, NKJV

Have you ever been pushed to the limit? And once you were, did you find that your limits were further than before? It never feels good to be tested in this way. It's uncomfortable and sometimes even painful. But it can be the best teacher if we allow it to push us to the brink while holding tight to our faith.

James was writing to Jewish believers, some likely scattered far from their homes and hunted down as believers of Jesus. Some betrayed by their own families and countrymen to the authorities. Falsely accused of crimes, imprisoned, even martyred for their faith and allegiance to Jesus.

As they listened or read the words James wrote, they might have felt the difficulties they faced would never end. But as they held onto the faith they received, the trials that pushed at them produced in them a valuable jewel; one they could use for every other discipline and virtue.

Patience is far undervalued in our culture today. Who wants to wait for anything anymore when you can have most anything now? But the best things worth having cannot be had without patience.

How can we love our children without it? Or live out our witness to our neighbors without the willingness to stick with it for the long haul? Or pray for our lost relatives, not knowing when we will see anything change, without patience?

Jesus didn't promise the road back to our Father wouldn't be bumpy. Quite the opposite; He promised peace in Him, but trouble in the world (John 16:33). Not a trouble to be avoided, but to be utilized. That if we hold onto the peace we have in our Father, He can use that trouble to perfect you and make you complete to be able to do His will (Hebrews 13:20-21).

Take some time to examine the trouble you have in your life. Whether it's trouble of your own making or not, how can you allow those circumstances to produce patience in you? Do you run from it, or hold to the faith and character Jesus is working into you? If you see a road ahead of you full of trials, you can know the destination will be a perfected faith if you hold firm to Him.

Notes:

_____

_____

_____

_____

_____

"If any of you lacks wisdom, let him ask of God, who gives to all liberally and without reproach, and it will be given to him. But let him ask in faith, with no doubting, for he who doubts is like a wave of the sea driven and tossed by the wind. For let not that man suppose that he will receive anything from the Lord; he is a double-minded man, unstable in all his ways."

– James 1:5-8, NKJV

I've heard about top level trainers, speakers, and entrepreneurs who would take their time to invest only in those who displayed a high level of commitment. Because their time was valuable to them, and they wished to use it wisely. And when put wisely in the right people the investment of knowledge they passed on would produce fruit in others.

You would think that if you received wisdom, it would change your life. And it can. But without the desire and drive to put it into practice, that timeless wisdom from the Timeless One will do you little good. Like when my parents told me to take care of my body so it didn't end up with unnecessary aches and pains later on. I took that wisdom passed down from those who had experience, and in my youthful ignorance did what I wanted instead. In hindsight, I could have saved myself some needless hardship.

There is a certain expectation we must have when coming to our Father. First, that we truly believe in Him; and second, He gives everything we need and more when we seek Him with everything we have (Hebrews 11:6). Being the kind of person who goes along with the flow will get you nowhere. Instead, like the captain of your *ship*, you must steer a course you wish to go in life. And when you need wisdom, you must be confident that your Father has it, He will give it, and that His wisdom is best.

Take some time to reaffirm your reliance on your Father. In your heart, mind, and soul the wisdom of the world must be regarded as substandard if it doesn't line up with His wisdom. Sometimes if we need instruction all we have to do is look around at what our Father has made. Everything He created displays wisdom, for those who have eyes to see it. *Now* is always an opportunity to ask the One who can give generously to those who will not doubt.

Notes:

_____

_____

_____

_____

_____

"Believers who are poor have something to boast about, for God has honored them. And those who are rich should boast that God has humbled them. They will fade away like a little flower in the field. The hot sun rises and the grass withers; the little flower droops and falls, and its beauty fades away. In the same way, the rich will fade away with all of their achievements."

— James 1:9-11, NLT

Have you ever felt you didn't fit in with others who were different from you? Maybe you were different in social status, ethnicity, traditions or even personality. It can be hard when you feel you don't fit in. And even if you are accepted, the feeling that you aren't can be hard to shake off.

At first, I felt James disliked rich people. As if he had the mentality that being poor as a Christian was a virtue to be attained over having wealth. But then I noticed he wasn't putting down people with money. Instead, he was putting them on equal footing as those who were poor.

Both the rich and the poor were to give glory back to God for what He had given them. Both had responsibilities. One had a responsibility to rely on God as their true source for provision of their needs to do the work He called them to. The other had a responsibility to rely on God as their true source for direction in allocating the resources He gave them for the work He called them to. Both needed to rely on their Father; and both were susceptible to forgetting they were in need. And neither of them was better.

We are all prone to holding judgements against others, even those we hardly know. But as adopted members of a new family we must all learn to live together as equals. Because we all were once sheep going our own way; but now our Father calls us to drink from the same river of life.

Take some time to check your heart for any wrongful judgements you may have against others. Maybe you dislike rich or poor people, or some other group. If you find any, repent and release them. If it's bitterness, release forgiveness and set yourself free. We as Christians are called to make righteous judgments (John 7:24, 1 Cor. 5; 6:2), but not to judge those outside our spiritual family, or other believers over petty differences. But if we are to err, let's err on the side of mercy over judgement (James 2:12-13).

Notes:

_____

_____

_____

_____

_____

"Blessed is the man who endures temptation; for when he has been approved, he will receive the crown of life which the Lord has promised to those who love Him. Let no one say when he is tempted, 'I am tempted by God'; for God cannot be tempted by evil, nor does He Himself tempt anyone. But each one is tempted when he is drawn away by his own desires and enticed. Then, when desire has conceived, it gives birth to sin; and sin, when it is full-grown, brings forth death."

— James 1:12-15, NKJV

Every tree in the forest began small. A small seed or sprout may seem insignificant, but leave it alone for decades and it will become a mighty tree with roots dug deep into the soil.

When we allow something to have control over any part of us, we give it permission to imprint itself onto us. When we were kids our parents molded us as authorities in our lives. Military boot camps mold you into a soldier ready for orders. And friendships, both good and bad, shape our future behavior.

The same is true for sin. When we allow it a place in our lives it latches itself onto us and slowly begins to grow until death is found hanging from its branches. Like a slow growing tree we don't see it right away. But over time as the roots entangle around our heart and the leaves show proof of what kind of tree it is, there can be little doubt what is happening.

If not for the work of the Master Gardener, this plant could never be pulled up and out of our hearts. But thankfully He specializes in tree and stump removal. Not only will He dig out all the death-producing sin, He will also plant His Spirit inside us. His Spirit begins to grow in us, changing us to be more like Him. He shows us how to ground the roots deeper into our hearts. He gives us tools to cultivate our hearts so the fruit of His planted Spirit will produce more.

Not only are we changed by the Master Gardener, but the seeds from His fruit can reproduce His life in others also.

Take some time to examine the ground of your heart. If you find sin, there is only One who can pluck it out of you. Ask your Father to weed out what is not from Him and begin to plant what will produce life in you. Then spend time cultivating your time with Him. As His life grows in you, you will see fruit. But don't hold it to yourself. It's always best to share what comes from your Father's garden.

Notes:

_____

_____

_____

_____

_____

"Do not be deceived, my beloved brethren. Every good gift and every perfect gift is from above, and comes down from the Father of lights, with whom there is no variation or shadow of turning. Of His own will He brought us forth by the word of truth, that we might be a kind of firstfruits of His creatures."

— James 1:16-18, NKJV

I used to give my kids money for them to put in the offering plate before they earned their own. It filled me with joy seeing them proudly put the money in, as if it were theirs to give. In that moment, they were pumped up with joy at having something to give and contribute.

We all tend to forget that every good thing we have comes from our Father. And what's more, we forget we received not just to use but also to give. We grow up, we go to a job that God provided, with the time He has given, with the talents and abilities He blessed us with, in the health He sustains us in and yet somehow our fingers close tightly around what rightly came from Him.

Everyone has been given talents and gifts, some latent and some blatant. But whether buried treasure or exposed, when God drew us to Him, He didn't do it for us to only be talented people. But rather He brought us in to become heirs with Him. And when you are an heir, you learn how to walk, talk, and live as your Father does. And your Father only gives good gifts.

If we believe what we have belongs to us, are we more at liberty to give, or less? Your Father puts things into your hand, heart, and head so you can bless, create, and make evident to all the kind of Father we belong to. When we choose to give away what isn't ours it fills us with joy. Why? Because it's more fun to give away what belongs to someone else, especially when He wants us to!

Giving what belongs to our Father causes us to turn back to Him again and again in wonder as our true source. When we have our eyes locked on Him, we can be fully confident that whatever we need He can give. And whatever others need, He can give to them also. And sometimes through us.

———————

Take some time, the time He gave you, and consider all that your Father has given you. He put resources in your hand to lay down as an offering to Him so you could experience part of His joy. If you have any part of your life that you are clinging onto as your own, then repent and give Him back ownership. Unclog your spiritual pipes and allow what belongs to your Father to flow through you to others once again. He has so much more to give through you, but the choice is yours.

Notes:

_____

_____

_____

_____

_____

For those who have planted seeds, you know that if given the right circumstances seeds tend to grow. A little bit of water, a little bit of dirt, and the right temperature range and you will likely see green sprouting. It's amazing that programmed within each seed is the capacity to grow into its parent. But before that seed in the bag can do anything some preparation is needed.

I've noticed that the more I set aside time with my Father to read, pray, and meditate on His words, the more I want to grow towards Him. But when I set aside less time, the less I want to. And the more I put myself in a healthy community of other believers, the more I want to live in accountability and invest in others. But when I withdraw from community, the less I want to contribute or to have my actions and lifestyle under scrutiny.

The difference between spiritually growing or spiritually declining is often determined by the preparations made beforehand. It is a result of what actions we take and where we put our time. Of what we say *yes* to, and of what we say *no* to.

A good father knows that giving his kids small responsibilities helps them to grow. And our Father gave you a responsibility in the form of caring for a seed. The seed is the life of Jesus being formed in you. The choice is ours what we do with it. We can nurture it and watch it sprout and grow. Or we can neglect it and abandon the costliest gift every given.

The only way to receive that seed is through the humility of repentance. We must admit we were wrong and turn from all those sins and lifestyles that defined our past. From that plant bed of humility Christ can be planted. And once we allow our old self to die, the life of Jesus can grow!

Take some time to garden your heart. Cultivate time away from distractions to be with your Father. Water your heart with His Word. Let His Spirit shine a light on your hidden times with Him so life can grow in and then out of you. And if you need help in your garden, always remember your Father loves it when you ask!

Notes:

_____

_____

_____

_____

_____

"But be doers of the word, and not hearers only, deceiving yourselves. For if anyone is a hearer of the word and not a doer, he is like a man observing his natural face in a mirror; for he observes himself, goes away, and immediately forgets what kind of man he was. But he who looks into the perfect law of liberty and continues in it, and is not a forgetful hearer but a doer of the work, this one will be blessed in what he does."

— James 1:22-25, NKJV

I tend to learn best when I am involved in a task. Someone can tell me or show me, but unless I put my hands to the task, I often forget. But when I am involved, I better understand not only the what's and how's, but also the whys.

The greatest thing ever done for us is contained in the good news of what Jesus did for us. We know what He did. He redeemed us by paying the price we should have paid. And we know how He did it. How He went to the cross, suffered, died, and on the third day rose again to life. But the part many don't fully understand or talk about is all the whys. We know it was because we were sinners needing saving so we could be with our Father again. But what about the other why's?

Why should we be *does of the word*? Wasn't the whole goal of the Gospel to set us free to be with our Father again? Or are we missing something?

James shows us that if we receive *the word of truth*, and it doesn't produce an action inside of us, we will be prone to forget who, and possibly Who's, we are. But the word of truth should cause action in our lives. Not actions that line up with our past lives, but with the new life from our Father. Because we weren't just saved *from* something; we were saved *for* something.

We weren't only saved because we needed it, even though we absolutely did. But because our Father had a higher calling for us. To live as sons and daughters of the only good Father. To be ambassadors of a higher kingdom. To be examples of a better way first shown to us by Jesus. And if we continue in actions that overflow from Him, and do not forget His word, we will be blessed in what we do.

Take some time to remember what you were saved from, and what you were saved for. Ask your Father to fill you once again with that joy of being saved from death. You don't have to earn anything; you've been given everything you need. And now you have freedom to act. To serve. To love others. To show by your actions that the love of the Father is the best motivation to living a life of freedom in Him.

Notes:

_____

_____

_____

_____

_____

"If anyone among you thinks he is religious, and does not bridle his tongue but deceives his own heart, this one's religion is useless. Pure and undefiled religion before God and the Father is this: to visit orphans and widows in their trouble, and to keep oneself unspotted from the world."

— James 1:26-27, NKJV

I used to live near Amish communities and loved watching the horse and buggies on the road. Loved it until I had to drive behind one, of course. But what I never saw was the carriage leading the horse. It was always the horse pulling the carriage. I'm sure the horse could push the carriage, but it wouldn't look right or work quite as well.

Our faith in Christ should bloom to look like a life of trust. Our words should sound like the voice of our Father. Our actions should look like the love of Jesus reaching down. Our good works can make a beautiful carriage. But if it is not pulled by love, purity, and a lifestyle of self-control, we may look like a horse trying to push a carriage.

Words have power. They can create or destroy. Build up or break down. If we master our mouth, we gain control over one of most powerful and useful tools in our arsenal. It can be used to encourage, build up, worship, and pray. To make declarations over you and your family that can last for generations. But out of control, our words can kindle a raging fire hard to put out.

Make no mistake, a lying tongue hates those it abuses. If you gossip, lie, or cheat someone, you hate them. Don't put a Christian spin on it. Those things are the opposite of love. And those who do those things are not operating in the heart of Christ who came to rescue the worst. Who came to free those living under the lie of the enemy by showing them the truth gift wrapped in His love. Who came to bring justice to those who have been cheated.

Many have made their own version of religion. While others disassociate themselves from anything religious. But true religion isn't bad, it just can't save you. Instead, you've been saved so you can freely practice your Father's version of religion. Your Father's idea of religion is to reach out to the most vulnerable in their time of greatest need. To go to the not-so-clean places, all while not allowing the world and its systems to corrupt what your Father is developing in you. When Jesus returns, let Him find us being *His* kind of religious, instead of our own.

Take some time to evaluate the words you've spoken recently. Have you spoken rashly instead of guarding what we say? Don't let the memories break you in shame. Instead, allow any guilt to be a catalyst for change. Bring any spoken failings to your Father. He has forgiveness if you have a penitent heart. Take that second, third, or even hundredth chance and turn it into an opportunity to try again!

Notes:

_____

_____

_____

_____

_____

"We then who are strong ought to bear with the scruples of the weak, and not to please ourselves. Let each of us please his neighbor for his good, leading to edification."

— Romans 15:1-2, NKJV

"Share each other's burdens, and in this way obey the law of Christ."

— Galatians 6:2, NLT

Hiking is often better when you have hiking buddies. The camaraderie and conversation make even a tough journey more bearable. It's tempting to walk on ahead if you are more skilled or fall behind if you are less skilled. But since you are both committed to reaching the same end, you both grow if you stick together.

If you have been to churches, you know how different we all are. It's truly amazing how a rag tag group from every ethnicity, every personality, and every age, can come together with a single focus and journey together to the cross. Many things in life show what divide us, but our Father brought us together and gave us an example of what in life can unite us.

Some come with baggage, slowly learning to trade their heavy pack for the Father's perfectly fitted one. Sanctification can be a rough process because change is never easy. But if we stay willing participants in the process, we will see growth. And if we carry the scars of being healed, we can help those who are still healing. But only if you walk together.

Some come not used to being part of a family and need to be shown what a family looks like. We all had different families; some good, some not so much, and some not there at all. But in the family of our Father all who come in the doorway of repentance can be a part. You can often spot them on the fringes, hesitant to get close or to be open. You can be the family they need, but only if you walk together.

If someone is a different age, you'll have to find ways to relate. If they are from a different culture, you'll have to find ways to communicate and share in the culture of Heaven. If we are strong in one area and they aren't, how would we be helping them if we chose not to walk together? But only if it is with humility, recognizing it is God who brings the change.

There is no end to our differences. There is no end to the stories we all have and the sins that were washed away. But if we follow our Father we can all walk together.

———————

Take some time to ask your Father to show you how you can share the burdens of your brothers and sisters. Ask Him for wisdom, and to develop humility in you for others. If God brings people to mind, pray for them. If He points them out, go and talk with them. Be family to them. Operating as a family is hard work but rewarding. Not being in a family is easy, but seldom do you grow.

Notes:

_____

_____

_____

_____

_____

> *"He gave five bags of silver to one, two bags of silver to another, and one bag of silver to the last – dividing it in proportion to their abilities. He then left on his trip."*
>
> *– Matthew 25:15, NLT*

I have fallen many times into the trap of comparing myself with the performance of others. Sometimes I would see those not doing much at all and complain inwardly that they should be doing more. Or at other times I would feel inadequate when I saw those operating at a high level of performance and question if I'm doing enough. Both approaches always left me trapped in comparison and kept me from fully using what I had been given.

The man in the story knew each of his servant's abilities before he gave them anything. He gave them what He knew they would be able to handle. In the same way your Father knows your abilities because He built them into you. He crafted you and knew your strengths and weaknesses. He pre-planned your initial giftings and abilities. And as you work with your Father He shapes and molds them during your life like raw, precious stones being refined. He doesn't expect you to reach someone else's potential. He is, however, looking for you to grow up to yours.

We aren't the judges of the productivity level of someone else's servants. What we are is stewards of whatever the Father has put into our hands. Some things we have been given are easier to recognize than others. Somethings are given to us over time. But with whatever we do have we should grow and foster it to gain more.

Just don't be like *that one guy*. The guy who knew what he had been given, and what he should do with it, but kept it from everyone. He didn't use it to gain more for his Master. He didn't even use his abilities a little bit at church services to gain interest and help others grow around him. He robbed not only his Master by his disobedient inactivity, but also all those who could have been blessed by the gifts of a loving Father through him.

Take some time to talk to your Father about what He has given you. What gifts is He shaping in you? What doors is He opening? What opportunities has He given you? If you don't know, ask your Father to open up your eyes to see what is in your hands. He may do it little by little, or all at once. And when you ask for wisdom, have no doubt in your mind that your generous Father will show it to you.

Notes:

_____

_____

_____

_____

_____

"If you are faithful in little things, you will be faithful in large ones. But if you are dishonest in little things, you won't be honest with greater responsibilities. And if you are untrustworthy about worldly wealth, who will trust you with the true riches of heaven? And if you are not faithful with other people's things, why should you be trusted with things of your own?"

— Luke 16:10-12, NLT

I love driving in the country and looking at all the farmlands. I often imagine all the things I would do if I had one plot of land or another. Would I reforest one area? Or maybe grow a garden or use animals to strengthen the soil. Or would I build an elaborate treehouse? The dreaming was fun. My imagination worked up many plans and thought up many possibilities.

But in the middle of all my daydreams, my Father asked me an irritating question: 'What are you doing with what you already have?'

Not that dreaming was the problem; our Father wants us to dream big. But at the time God was refocusing me on what was in my hands and what I was doing with what He had given. We can't do much with what is outside of our hands, but we can with what is. And if I am not faithful with what is already in my care, why should I be given more?

One of the best ways to develop a passion for what God has given you is to be faithful with it. When you are faithful with what has been placed in your hands you give it your time. You care and nurture it. Your actions begin to shape its future and plant prophetic seeds for how it can be better. You see where it is and where it can be. And if you keep your Father's heart for that area, you will catch a part of His vision for it.

We all have our own idea of what our spiritual career path will look like. But our Father often has different plans on how we will grow. He puts things in our path to help shape us. Will we lean on His guidance? Will we give our full effort into what is in front of us?

Too often we see things in our lives as tests to be taken. And sometimes that can be partially true. But more often I believe what God brings our way has far more in common with on-the-job training. Instead of wondering if we passed a test, we should ask if we were faithful with what was put in front of us.

Take some time to evaluate what is in your hands. What has your Father put in your life right now to be faithful with? And how are you being faithful to learn and grow while you work? Our Father loves to take us on as apprentices and walk with us in the areas He has created for us to walk in. And as you serve faithfully, remember to draw on His strength and wisdom so you can grow.

Notes:

_____

_____

_____

_____

_____

"David said, 'My son Solomon is still young and inexperienced. And since the Temple to be built for the Lord must be a magnificent structure, famous and glorious throughout the world, I will begin making preparations for it now.' So David collected vast amounts of building materials before his death."

– 1 Chronicles 22:5, NLT

Every parent wants their kids to have it better than they did. We want them to have everything they need to be successful. But what if we focused more on passing on skills, tools, and resources so they can build, instead of giving them something already built?

How many failures could we have avoided if we had been prepared to meet those challenges? Struggle and failure can be good teachers. But passing along wisdom gained from experience puts the starting line further down the track so smaller obstacles won't derail the unprepared.

One day, those much younger than us will grow and face their own challenges. But what can we as fathers, mothers, or mentors, do so they can rise to new levels? It is a beautiful thing to prepare provisions for those going after us. Not provisions enabling work avoidance, but rather tools and skills they can use to build something far greater than we could have ever imagined.

Long ago, another Father paved the way for those who would go after. He gave the best gifts! The greatest was His own Son. Entrusted with the responsibility of being a living example of a royal Heir, the Son showed how we could be adopted into this family. For hundreds of years this Father prepared the world for the greatest example of what He was like.

The Father's Son gave us many tools we could use, and instructions on how to use them. Even when the ultimate sacrifice was needed, the Son was willing to lay His life down so we could have all the provisions we needed for the future. But even then, the Father didn't leave us all alone. He sent another gift for us to have: His Spirit. His Spirit inside us made us heirs also to an unseen, yet growing, kingdom. His Spirit reminded us of the lessons we were taught and gave wisdom and direction in how to use them. Until one day when we will receive another gift: reunification with our Father.

Take some time to think about how you are preparing those younger than you for their future. Not only your own children, but all those you cross paths with. What valuable lessons could you show them? What wisdom have you learned? And perhaps most importantly, you could show others how they can get back to the loving Father: by showing them the way to His Son.

Notes:

_____

_____

_____

_____

_____

"'My thoughts are nothing like your thoughts,' says the Lord. 'And my ways are far beyond anything you could imagine. For just as the heavens are higher than the earth, so my ways are higher than your ways and my thoughts higher than your thoughts. The rain and snow come down from the heavens and stay on the ground to water the earth. They cause the grain to grow, producing seed for the farmer and bread for the hungry.'"

– Isaiah 55:8-10, NLT

When I give my kids advice, they, like most kids, don't always want to take it. Mainly because they don't understand it. In their minds what I'm saying makes no sense. To them it is an untested, unproven concept. In some cases, they only take bits and pieces of my advice, and don't get the desired result and therefore dismiss it, saying 'it doesn't work.' But if they were to continue putting it into practice, they would see a much different result.

When we first hear about our Father's ways, they seem foreign and strange to us. The natural mind wants to dismiss it as fantasy. Love your enemy? Do good to those who are mistreating you? Fast and pray? We have to be a servant to others to become great? It seems to make no sense from a logical perspective. And they may never make sense until we begin to put them into practice and see the fruit.

When we begin putting God's ways into practice, those ways eventually seem less strange and become more familiar. Because the ways our Father gave us are how we were created to operate. The wholeness that comes out of this newfound life begins a healing work in every area of our lives. And soon the strange ways of God become the life-giving ways of God.

When God opens our minds and hearts and begins the process of changing us from the inside out, then we understand His ways are the best ways. But this process of revelation can often take time. And until we have the curtain pulled back, He asks that we trust Him to do things His way.

Take some time to ask your Father to show you more of His ways. Ask for the curtain to be pulled back so you can begin understanding His ways. But also, ask Him to point out areas you can grow in obedience. We don't have to always understand His ways. Sometimes that comes with Him showing it to us, and sometimes it comes with exercising our obedience over time. Either way, our Father stands with hand outstretched, ready to walk it out with us. Will you trust Him?

Notes:

_____

_____

_____

_____

_____

"For the weapons of our warfare are not carnal but mighty in God for pulling down strongholds, casting down arguments and every high thing that exalts itself against the knowledge of God, bringing every thought into captivity to the obedience of Christ."

— 2 Corinthians 10:4-5, NKJV

When I hike, one of the greatest things that saps my resolve to finish is my own attitude. If my thoughts go astray and I begin to focus on the difficulty or how much my body aches, the more I want to quit. I start to lose sight of the finish line and what it takes to get there. And even if I don't quit, I would feel miserable the whole way up. Self-control over the mind is key to any hike preparation.

It is the same as preparing ourselves for daily life. Because in our daily life there is an invisible war raging around us. The prize of this war is your heart, mind, and soul. The ammunition used comes in the form of words, both spoken and in the mind. And the weapons that use this ammunition are limitless in form.

The devil wars with ideas, arguments, and questions filled with doubt. He has limited power and must use subterfuge to redirect with a false narrative and ideas of who God is and the world He created.

What we allow to germinate and stay in our minds will grow. If you want a healthy mind, you must do weed control. We must learn to recognize these subtle and spiritually subversive ideas in our own mind first and confront them there before those seeds grow.

We must actively speak truth over anything, every idea, every argument, or conversation that would try and plant ideas that turn us away from the knowledge of Christ. And every thought that says, 'did God really say?' Every creative structure with a narrative that pits itself against the knowledge of Christ and discovering Him.

We are battling against the world system, not the people in the world. If the words or ideas coming from others match the worldly system, it is important to use the grace, wisdom, and timing God gives us when we bring truth. Because it is God's goodness, not just bringing truth, that leads us to repentance (Romans 2:4). But if we out of a sense of kindness take no stand at all and withhold loving actions or words that bring our Father's grace, are we truly being kind? But let everything we do be motivated by the love of our Father.

———————

Take some time to check if you have any wrong thoughts, ideas, or narratives you have allowed to take residence in your mind. Ask your Father to point out anything that is blocking you from coming to a better knowledge or level of intimacy with Him. We have all picked up *thought-baggage* in our journey through life. But once our loving Father points it out then it's time to speak truth over ourselves until His truth sets us free.

Notes:

_____

_____

_____

_____

_____

"My brethren, do not hold the faith of our Lord Jesus Christ, the Lord of glory, with partiality."

— James 2:1, NKJV

"Owe nothing to anyone except to love one another, for the one who loves his neighbor has fulfilled the Law."

— Romans 13:8, NASB

Is the reason we have greeters at our churches to make people feel welcome, or to abdicate our own responsibility to show love to others? Have we reduced the command of greeting our spiritual siblings to a simple word or nod in passing, or do we take hospitality seriously?

I used to skim over the last parts of Paul's epistles to the house churches that were spread across the Roman empire. Yet a very consistent command always hid near the end in plain sight: Greet your family! It seemed odd at first. But in order to grow together they needed to be willing to unite with everyone the Father drew into the family.

It is a call to action on the part of believers as a debt of love to our fellow siblings. This love was to be shown regardless of position, class, race, or social status. It called both rich and poor to live as members of a kingdom not of this world.

I used to be confused why Jesus told His disciples not to greet anyone on the road when He sent them out in Luke 10. It made me think that greeting had to be far more than a simple salutation in passing. It must have involved time and energy in conversation. This picture of investment in Christian community is what we are to live up to. But are there people we are unwilling to invest in with this kind of greeting?

There are certain kinds of people we naturally gravitate towards. Certain personalities mesh better. People with similar interests and backgrounds tend to get along better. All these things are natural.

But we are called to go against human nature and take on the nature of our Father. We are called to esteem our new family over our own nationalities, social ranking, and race. And this requires us to step outside our comfort zone and greet those in our new family.

———

Take some time to get to know a brother or sister in Christ who is different than you in some way. Greet them. Honor them. Spend quality time interacting. And remember, whatever you do for the least of your brothers and sisters, you do for our greatest sibling, Jesus.

Notes:

_____

_____

_____

_____

_____

"The Lord brings the counsel of the nations to nothing; He makes the plans of the peoples of no effect. The counsel of the Lord stands forever, the plans of His heart to all generations."

— Psalm 33:10-11, NKJV

When my kids come to me with their next great plan, I often offer my advice. They would listen at times, but at other times they had everything all figured out and couldn't possibly be wrong. As a father, I want so much to step in to help their plans, and sometimes do. But sometimes I find it best to let things play out so they learn a life lesson.

Do you want to make plans that will change the world for multiple generations? Then as a royal heir with special access to the limitless wisdom of the Father, ask for counsel in your plans. Do you want to give rock solid advice? Then take the opinions of your Father and let them become you own.

Before you were born, your heart was uniquely shaped and created. Like a piece to a puzzle, you were designed to display a picture to the world of who your Father is. A work of art with the fingerprints of the Great Artist. But sin corrupted our hearts and stained the image we were created to display.

But the Father had a plan. His plan was to make a way for you to be adopted into His family again (Ephesians 1:5). He planned for all those who were adopted to carry the family secrets and share them with everyone (Matt. 10:26-27). His plan was for all His adopted children to become more like Him by first being like His firstborn Son (Romans 8:28-30).

These plans, and many others, were prepared in advance, awaiting the day for you to come back home. Everything was prepared, your room was ready with all the stuff you would need. Your place at the table was set. The only thing missing was you coming home. And once you do, you get activated into the family business of bringing other orphans to their new home.

Take some time to ask your Father His advice and counsel on issues you are dealing with. You may have to quiet your mind and heart to hear His voice. He won't give you bad advice, even if it is advice we don't want to hear. But the real test will be if we are willing to put it into practice.

Notes:

_____

_____

_____

_____

_____

"You love righteousness and hate wickedness; Therefore God, Your God, has anointed You with the oil of gladness more than Your companions."

– Psalm 45:7, NKJV

"Seek good and not evil, that you may live; so the Lord God of hosts will be with you, as you have spoken. Hate evil, love good; establish justice in the gate."

– Amos 5:14-15a, NKJV

Has your love for something ever stirred an equally matched hate for something else? Or do you believe that as followers of Christ we should never hate? To understand why God hates sin so much we must first understand what He loves, and why He loves what He does.

God loves us and couldn't imagine a world apart from us. But sin entered the world through deception and disobedience, putting a chasm between us and Him, dooming us as children to eternity without our Father.

All of us, to one measure or another, have added to the cause of this separation by our sins; breaking away from our Father and breaking His heart. Wounding others. Even stealing from others the blessings they could have received if we had lived up to our destiny as sons and daughters of our Father. The smallest infraction all the way up to the ugliest, dirtiest, and most shameful parts of all human existence had to be brought to justice. And because God also deeply loves justice, a price had to be paid.

But our heavenly Dad from the very beginning had a plan. To bridge the chasm and once again be reunited with us He had to sacrifice something He loved. The perfect Father had to give up His perfect Son to bring His imperfect children back.

If God loved us that much, and loved his Son that much, and loves justice that much, then how much must He hate sin? And how much must He hate injustice? Pure love drove our Father to action. Does it drive you to action as well? A casual affinity towards others might make you care or feel bad for them, but if the pure love of our Father lives in you it will compel you to action.

What if we hated sin like we hate cancer, but loved sinners like a beloved family member who had that disease? We would walk with them through any ordeal until the plague was wiped from their body. We would celebrate every victory, mourn every defeat, and be present for every need. What would the world see if believers loved like that? They just might see the hands and feet of their Father.

Notes:

_____

_____

_____

_____

_____

"Now after the death of Jehoiada the leaders of Judah came and bowed down to the king. And the king listened to them. Therefore they left the house of the Lord God of their fathers, and served wooden images and idols; and wrath came upon Judah and Jerusalem because of their trespass. Yet He sent prophets to them, to bring them back to the Lord; and they testified against them, but they would not listen."

— 2 Chronicles 24:17-19, NKJV

Along the side of a path, I saw a large, mostly decayed stump. Once a grand tree, the stump was now slowly decaying into the soil, giving the last of its life to the trees that would follow. I stood amazed as I realized that we, like trees, can have a lasting effect long after we are gone. And that the best way to honor those who have had a positive example on you is to emulate that change in our own lives.

Have you ever had someone very influential in your life removed from you? And after they weren't there anymore, did you continue living out the example left to you, or revert to old habits or sins? Grief over a loss can throw us off track; and in our vulnerability we are more at risk to follow lesser examples. If you find yourself in this situation, be careful who you allow to speak into your life. Take the time to grieve and remember what was passed on to you.

Although they may be gone from you, their example and words can live on in you. Not to become someone other than who you are, but to grow in character and become who our Father has called you to be.

The question is, will we allow the legacy of those who have gone before to speak into us? Are we willing to carry an encouraging word and a listening ear? And to be the role model who points others back to their Father and reminds them to make room to hear from Him.

Take some time to remember the legacy handed down to you. Have you allowed those positive examples to speak through you to others? Even if you don't have a good example to point to, you can always look to the example of Jesus. He gave all of Himself and is an example worth following. He gave us a chance to come back to the Father who never gave up on us. All because He chose to give of Himself and leave a legacy to those who would follow.

Notes:

_____

_____

_____

_____

_____

"But King David replied to Araunah, 'No, I insist on buying it for the full price. I will not take what is yours and give it to the Lord. I will not present burnt offerings that have cost me nothing!'"

— *1 Chronicles 21:24, NLT*

When I was a teenager, I worked to save up for my first car. It took me a while, but I was able to pay cash for it. It wasn't the greatest car, but I loved it! I would baby it and clean it meticulously. I was careful how I drove it, at least for a while. I even gave it a name! It had cost me dearly, and because of that cost it became dear to me.

Your heart will follow what you treasure. Your *treasure* can come in many forms. Your time, thoughts, energy, gifts, all your stuff, each are currency in your hands. Each day we spend them on what is dear to us, and what we wish to become dear to us. And because all these are in our hands, the temptation is to forget where they come from.

If we were honest with ourselves, we would see that everything we have is not truly ours. Our time on earth is not guaranteed. Our health and energy are never a certainty. Circumstances can change. But while we have something to give, what will we choose to do with it?

If we do not recognize that all we have belongs to God, we are less likely to use them for Him. Do we give Him the best of who we are, or our leftover energy? What do we need to lay down that is costly to us and allow it to be God's possession again? It always was. But enough time holding tightly to the belongings of our Father can sometimes make us forget.

Why is obedience better than sacrifice? Why does our Father want us to have mercy and a knowledge of Him more than sacrifice? Because the greatest thing we can give is ourselves. When we obey our Father and show mercy, and learn His ways, we begin to be a living sacrifice. Sacrificing our old, childish selves so we look more like our Heavenly Dad. We become ready to lay down everything we have been given. Not only do we become a part of His family again, but our Father finally gets to see us use His stuff that He put in our hands.

———————

Take some time to take something costly to you and give ownership back to where it belongs. Ask your Father what inside of you needs to be laid down so He can use it again. This could be your time or resources. Whatever it is, be willing to lay it down. Your Father can do incredible things with His gifts that He put inside of us, if we are willing to follow His lead and use them in partnership with Him.

Notes:

_____

_____

_____

_____

_____

"Look after each other so that none of you fails to receive the grace of God. Watch out that no poisonous root of bitterness grows up to trouble you, corrupting many."

— Hebrews 12:15, NLT

As a boy I remember seeing my grandfather work in his garden. He had farmed his whole life, and I enjoyed watching him work. As we passed a tree growing in the front yard, he noticed a small sprout forming on the side of the trunk. Without explanation he used his thumb to break the sprout off. I didn't understand until years later why he did this.

Do you handle problems when they are small, or wait until they are too big to ignore? We all have done it. Sometimes out of avoidance; sometimes procrastination. Often hoping our problems would go away by themselves.

Life actively happens to us every day. People, groups, and organizations make choices all the time. Some we like, and some we don't. Both hurtful words and harmful actions can be taken against us. And with each negative encounter we have a choice. Do you choose to forgive and move forward when the wound is freshly sprouted, or remain stuck in unforgiveness until the root grows into a tangled jungle?

What about those who have suffered tremendous wounds and had unspeakable hurts from others? Forgiveness is no easy task for those who have had so much wrong committed against them. But thankfully our Father did not leave us without a healing trail to follow. When we were at our worst, our Father sent His best, His Son Jesus. And to those who carry heavy burdens from living in this world, He offers to carry our pack for us (Matt. 11:28-30). We then get to choose to give it over to Him or continue to carry it. It may seem impossible to forgive sometimes, but with our Father all things are possible (Matt. 19:26).

There is a popular lie we should avoid. Time does not bring healing. But your Father does. And the choices you make during that time with Him will determine your freedom. There is no magic timeline for how long it should take either. But the principle remains. What you let fester over time will grow. But what you uproot clears room for planting something new.

Take some time to check your heart for bitterness, resentment, and unforgiveness. If you find any, ask your Father to give you the wisdom to uproot these from your life. Some may be easier than others. If you don't feel ready, then be honest with your Father and ask Him to work on your heart and bring you to a place of healing. He may ask you to take a hard step. But it will be worth it when new life begins to sprout in you again!

Notes:

_____

_____

_____

_____

"I am the true grapevine, and my Father is the gardener."

— John 15:1, NLT

Have you ever seen the process of grafting in a new branch? It's an amazing process! The receiving tree must be cut in preparation for the new branch. The new branch must also be cut out of its former tree and trimmed to fit into the slot made in the new tree. Once put into place, the branch and tree are wrapped together until they grow as one.

This is what happens to those who become united with their Father. We all used to belong to other dying trees, but because of the love of the Master Gardener, He made a way for us to be joined to the Tree of life.

The Master Gardener saw all the branches out there attached to roots of sin, choked by weeds and decay. He knew without intervention what the end would be. But He had a plan. A plan He worked out when He first made His garden. But it would involve cutting the Tree He loved, His first Tree.

The Master Gardener closed His eyes, picturing what He was about to do. He gazed between His Tree and all the dying branches, and with love in His heart but pain in His eyes began making cuts into His most loved Tree.

He counted each notch, making sure there was room for every branch that wanted to be joined. He watched as His beautiful Tree began looking more mutilated with every cut. But with purpose and determination continued.

With every cut made, the Master was ready. One by one, all the willing branches were cut from the dying trees. Each branch He trimmed and shaped for a specific spot. Then with great care, the Master Gardener joined branch and Tree and covered over the brokenness of the branch with wrap, not to be uncovered until the life of the Tree brought healing and unity.

The Master Gardener gave the branch one more loving touch, then waited for both to grow together. He would not leave them alone; His great love kept Him close to watch every minute. He had poured everything He had into His Tree, and now through His Tree He could bring life to all.

Take some time to reflect on the great gift you have been given of being united back to the Father through Jesus. It was a gift, not a right. Not earned by merit but offered out of love. It isn't a sign of a Father continually angry, but proof of a Father fighting for His kids and giving everything He had to win them back. This one truth is enough for us to give all our thanks to the Master Gardener. He isn't asking us to pay Him back, just that we would grow in Him.

Notes:

_____

_____

_____

_____

_____

"He cuts off every branch of mine that doesn't produce fruit, and he prunes the branches that do bear fruit so they will produce even more."

— John 15:2, NLT

Don't waste time holding on to what God has destined for the trim pile. Do you see limitations as opportunities for growth to spring through? If God is reducing your avenues, do you see it as an opportunity for better growth?

The God of limitless life and power sees what can be produced in us and will trim away all the extra branches so even the small growth He sees in us can accelerate. He takes away the clutter so the pure can shine through. He takes away the extra, even when it is good, so He can draw out the great.

But when we feel God pruning branches out of us, are we prepared to let go? Some of the branches have been with us for a long time and hurt to let go. Others are new growth, and we recover quickly from the loss. It is a test of our trust in our Father, that as the Master Gardener He knows best how to draw the most out of you.

We sometimes have a hard time thinking that God wants less so He can bring more. We have our minds set that He brings more so we will have more. Some think God only operates in addition. But He often subtracts so that He can multiply.

Are we too busy with tasks that don't produce anything? Have we been saying yes to busily serving in so many areas that we miss the *great* that God wants to draw out of us? If so, it might be about pruning time. And that might mean learning to say no a little more so we are prepared to say yes to what God has for us.

Take some time to identify which areas God has called you to be focused on. Then put everything else in a separate pile as optional, even if some are good. We all have limited time in life, and each of us has been given an area of influence. Ask your Father if any of those things have become a distraction to what He wants to grow in you, and trust that He will show you. If He points any out, be prepared to prune back.

Notes:

_____

_____

_____

_____

_____

"You are already clean because of the word I have spoken to you."

— John 15:3, NKJV

After a long hike up a dusty trail, one reward I can seldom pass on is soaking my feet in a lake or stream. All the dirt washes away and I feel brand new!

There is another stream we need to wash and soak in daily. One that never runs dry because it flows from the best source: straight from the heart and mouth of our Father.

What goes in will come out. If you fill yourself with garbage, garbage will eventually come out. We know this almost instinctively, and yet we still catch ourselves soaking negative thoughts, words, and ideas into our minds and hearts. We are sponges, and when squeezed, we will gush out what is inside. We need a pure source to flush out the sewage that has made our hearts grow septic. More than just positivity, we need pure, life-giving water.

In comes the beautiful cycle of our Father's Word! Out of the overflow of His heart He spoke His Word into life. When we fill ourselves with God's living and active word, we are filling ourselves with the heart of the Father. And when we fill our hearts with His words, our hearts will overflow with His words also. And when His words bubble up from our hearts it can produce life in us and those around us to repeat the cycle!

Take some time to cycle into your heart the words of the Father. Ask God to soften your heart so you can see and understand something new from what you read. If possible, find a consistent time to regularly fill your heart and mind. But also ask your Father to identify the negative sources that should be cut out. Our Father knows each of us individually and knows what should stay and what should go. He won't overload you all at once. He is patient and is willing to walk this out with you no matter how long it takes.

Notes:

_____

_____

_____

_____

_____

*"The generous will prosper; those who refresh
others will themselves be refreshed."*

— Proverbs 11:25, NLT

*"Love your enemies! Do good to them. Lend to them without
expecting to be repaid. Then your reward from heaven will be very
great, and you will truly be acting as children of the Most High,
for He is kind to those who are unthankful and wicked. You must
be compassionate, just as your Father is compassionate."*

— Luke 6:35-36, NLT

We all have a choice between two kinds of people. Those who sit and inwardly complain that no one reaches out to them, or those who look for opportunities to reach out. We all want to think of ourselves as the second kind, but when it comes to walking it out, many times we are more like the first.

Every action we take is practice for our future. Whatever we do is training for us to do it again. When we sit and complain, we train ourselves to be better at sitting and complaining. But even when we fumble forward while doing something good, we've at least trained ourselves how to do it better the next time.

Sitting and complaining is easy. But being involved even when we don't know what to do is hard. But the longer we take to act only reinforces our old ways of not acting. If we wait until we feel like reaching out, we might never do it. Our Father never called us to feel a certain way, but to act a certain way. And when we do reach out to serve, we often find that our feelings will follow.

Even imperfect practice is practice. We all start somewhere, and there is no better time to start practicing than right now. You will face setbacks, and not every situation will feel comfortable, but the effort will be worth it in the end.

―――――

Take some time to begin imperfectly reaching out to others. Think of who you can bless today. Who might need a neighbor, or a listening ear? Can you offer encouragement to someone? Are you willing to be the kind of person you want others to be to you? It doesn't have to be perfect. Just be genuine and watch yourself become more like a child of the Most High.

Notes:

_____

_____

_____

_____

_____

"To everything there is a season, a time for every purpose under heaven."

— Ecclesiastes 3:1, NKJV

Have you ever wondered why God sometimes takes good things out of your life? We know everything has a season, but it can be hard when we must let some things go.

Sometimes our Father takes good things out of our lives because they were only meant to be in our lives for a season. Probably to teach us something and then move on. And then, like the lowest branches on an ever-growing tree, they slowly fade and fall away. Or it might be something that was not meant to be in our lives, or wrong timing, and God mercifully withdraws it to keep us focused.

It could be that we have elevated that good thing to the level of idolatry and made it our source instead of our Father. Other times it may be that we have placed part, or all, our identity in that good thing instead of keeping our identity simply as a son or daughter of our Father.

There is so little in life that we need. When we come to this realization it is incredibly liberating. And when good things come and go, we can be content in knowing God is our source and will bring into our lives what we really need. But that doesn't mean we should stop asking. Our Father encourages us to ask of Him and loves to give good gifts.

As we grow in relationship with our Father, He wants us to grow our trust in Him. This process produces maturity because exercising our trust usually means exercising our faith in Him by taking difficult steps. When our trust grows in our Father, so does our confidence to walk boldly into the unknown with Him. Even if that means letting go of what He is taking away.

Take some time to list the good God has brought into your life. Spend time thanking your Father for each of those things. But hold them loosely in your hand and never let them take the place of our true source. Some things may stay, and some may go. But the Giver of all good things will never leave you.

Notes:

_____

_____

_____

_____

_____

"Oh, that My people would listen to me! Oh, that Israel would follow Me, walking in My paths! How quickly I would then subdue their enemies! How soon My hands would be upon their foes!"

– Psalm 81:13-14, NLT

I love the sounds of nature when they are undiluted with the noises we usually hear. What always hits me is how loud those gentle sounds become when I allow myself to be quiet and listen. And when I come back down from the mountain, I notice my ears had become tuned to hear those same sounds. My *normal world* had become alive with sounds I had slowly learned to ignore.

If we are honest, most of us surround ourselves with noise. The noise of activity, of media, and of busyness. To some, silence seems scary and they seek to drown out the beautiful silence with the clutter of noise. But when we do, we are robbing ourselves of something valuable: a chance to hear the still, small voice of our Father.

We have the opportunity each day to train the ears of our soul. We can train them to listen, or to tune things out. But why would we tune out an opportunity to hear from a Father Who loves us? Could it be that we are afraid of what He will say? Or of what He will ask of us? These thoughts betray a belief that our ways are better than God's ways. But over and over our Father pleads with us that if we both hear and follow Him, He can set things right in our lives.

So how do we practice listening? Practicing stillness is a great way to start giving room for God to speak. Even in busy times we can practice having that stillness with Him. In that stillness He brings a peace that only He can give, and no one can take away unless we give it away.

Once we experience that peace, why would anyone want to abandon it? Most of us wouldn't say: 'I don't want God's peace'. But our actions speak louder when we don't foster our inner ear in the place of quietness. But like any good habit, it must be nurtured to grow.

———

Take some time to slow down and intentionally practice stillness as if you were sitting face to face with your Father. This will require patience as we slowly grow accustomed to the quiet. This can be in your devotion times but can also be practiced in other areas of our lives. Ask your Father to speak with you and make room in your heart to listen by allowing Him the opportunity to speak. If you allow room for consistent quiet times where your Father can speak with you, I know He will!

Notes:

_____

_____

_____

_____

_____

"They also acquired and imported from Egypt a chariot for six hundred shekels of silver, and a horse for one hundred and fifty, thus, through their agents, they exported them to all the kings of the Hitties and the kings of Syria."

— 2 Chronicles 1:17, NKJV

I often look for opportunities for my kids to learn a new skill or gain more understanding when it comes to the marketplace. Most parents probably do the same thing. We want our kids to be successful with whatever gifts our Father put inside them. But our God-given talents aren't the only gifts to focus on. We also have been given time and opportunities.

The opportunities we find in the marketplace can be used to bless both you and those around you. Everywhere we look ordinary things can be turned into marketable ideas, inventions, and innovations. God wants to use every area of life to bring His blessing into the earth. Your sensitivity to God's gifting in your life can be used to find these opportunities if your ear is tuned to Him.

Whatever area you find yourself in can be used as a conduit for God's ways to bring renewal. Because when His ways are put into place His blessings can flow. The change God wants to bring might be structural, so a business operates more in line with His heart for others. He might also give insight into procedures that could save money and increase productivity or bring a better work/life balance to your employees.

Time is a gift we can't keep. It can only be spent. We don't know how much of it we have, and we can't keep it in our hands anyway. So why not use it so time can work on your side? One important way is to invest in people early, and often. Or to not wait years to flush out an idea God is giving you. To stop only thinking and begin doing. It's ok to start small; your Father loves watching your first steps.

Work is a beautiful word. It produces, creates, brings life, and takes what used to not exist and brings it into being. If God began with work what makes us think it would be any different for us since we are made in His image? He has work for us both now and in the age to come.

———————————

Take some time to ask your Father to help you recognize the opportunities around you. But also ask yourself how you are using what God has given you. If you aren't using God's gifts He gave you now, then you likely won't receive more to use later. Ask your Father for opportunities to use your gifting to be a blessing. He is eagerly waiting for you to become His business partner in His mission!

Notes:

_____

_____

_____

_____

_____

"Then the messenger who had gone to call Micaiah spoke to him, saying, 'Now listen, the words of the prophets with one accord encourage the king. Therefore please let your word be like the word of one of them, and speak encouragement.' And Micaiah said, 'As the Lord lives, whatever my God says, that I will speak.'"

— 2 Chronicles 18:12-13, NKJV

What kinds of words do you listen to? Do you allow yourself to internalize a challenge brought to you? Or, like far too many, do you only listen to what makes you feel good?

There is a season for everything. Sometimes you need encouragement. Sometimes conviction, knowledge, or wisdom in deciding a course of action. But if the only voices you let speak to you are encouraging ones, then you may become stunted spiritually, relationally, and emotionally.

There are times when we all need to hear the word no. There are times to be told that what we are doing is wrong or harmful. If we are never challenged, then how will we grow? And if we distance ourselves from those who can challenge us, we limit those opportunities for growth.

Iron can only sharpen iron by friction and close contact. In the same way those who are willing to speak truth in love into your life should be kept close. Those are the people you should value the most because they will draw the most growth out of you.

Correction is hard to accept. It stings our pride and wounds our false image of ourselves. Healthy correction and rebukes are like strong winds against a rickety hut. The wind may knock it down, but better to be tested and collapse before our construction is over our own heads. And those that bring loving correction show a belief that our hands are capable of building something far greater.

Take some time to separate all your friends into groups. Groups that challenge you out of love, those that don't challenge you, and those who challenge but not out of love. Those that don't challenge you can be encouraging but recognize there may be areas they won't be able to help you with. Those who challenge you but not out of love learn to develop healthy boundaries with. They may have good advice, but since their delivery may be harmful those boundaries will help better sift the good from the bad.

But those who have a heart to help with the challenging words they bring should be kept close. They will sharpen you as you spend time with them. Value their words, but don't forget to weigh them. And no matter how good or encouraging, never accept anything that doesn't align with the words of your Father. Because His words over you are the most important.

Notes:

_____

_____

_____

_____

_____

*"And when He had sent the multitudes away, He went
up on the mountain by Himself to pray."*

— Matthew 14:23a, NKJV

Do you struggle finding the time for devotions? Do situations in life pull at you until you end up with no time left? For many, this is a reality of life. Sometimes by choice, sometimes by circumstance.

If you find yourself in this situation often as I have, then here is a secret for you: we all are given 24 hours a day, and 7 days a week. Everyone is allotted this portion and asked to be stewards of it. Everyone is a manager of their time.

This reality is scary. We don't want to think about it this way because it places the entirety of the blame on us for how we manage our time. There is no condemnation if temporary circumstances really do restrict our time; I've been there many times. But if the excuse that you have no time keeps ringing out, after a while it will ring hollow.

Jesus often left huge crowds of people, people who came only to see and hear from Him, to spend time alone with His Father. Imagine if a world leader took a step back for a few hours or days because he needed guidance from God. Hopefully a part of us would want to cheer him on for being a godly leader. But probably a small part of us might also be tempted to hold offense and accuse him of leaving his responsibilities.

The principle is this: without consistent time with our Father we will be of little good to those around us and to our destiny. Jesus humbled Himself and relied on His Father's guidance to fulfill His destiny. And if we want to see ours, we would be wise to follow in His steps.

Take some time to be with your Father. Are we willing to make room for Him? Can we say no to some meaningless things to make room for the one who gives us meaning? The beautiful thing is your Father isn't forcing you to be with Him; even though He desperately wants you to be. Without Him we can do nothing (John 15:5), but with Him we can do all things (Philippians 4:13). Too much time away from Him will sap you dry, but in Him is life.

Notes:

_____

_____

_____

_____

_____

"Now, most people would not be willing to die for an upright person, though someone might perhaps be willing to die for a person who is especially good. But God showed His great love for us by sending Christ to die for us while we were still sinners."

— Romans 5:7-8, NLT

Have you ever felt racked with guilt for messing up and failing in your daily journey with Jesus? Maybe you have guilt and shame from your past life that peeks its head around every corner of your mind. In many ways, these thoughts can keep you from the greatest joys of life with your Father and from fulfilling your purpose on this earth.

For some it needs to be a perspective shift. Healthy guilt drives us to Jesus for forgiveness, but lingering shame can tear the strongest down. We must remember it wasn't just because of us that Christ died, but for us. Like a hero battling it out until he won back his bride from the enemy, so Jesus humbled himself, came down and went through death and hell to win us back.

Our response to being rescued from certain death and eternal separation should be one of life-changing gratitude and devotion. You've not only been rescued, but you've also been adopted into a family (Galatians 4:4-5). Your sins, and all the junk of the past, Jesus purchased by buying out your debt. His actions created an unending, unlimited grant for anyone who wants it. It's free, but it will cost you everything.

Take some time to meditate on what God has done for you, and the great price that was paid for you. But instead of dwelling on shame, focus on the fact that Jesus came to win and redeem you back. He thought you were worth it then, and still does. And now you can live the calling He has for you. What will you do now that you have a clean slate? What will you do now that you have a new Father and family in Christ?

Notes:

_____

_____

_____

_____

_____

"But we have this treasure in earthen vessels, that the excellence of the power may be of God and not of us."

— 2 Corinthians 4:7, NKJV

"I, therefore, the prisoner of the Lord, beseech you to walk worthy of the calling with which you were called."

— Ephesians 4:1, NKJV

Imagine you agreed to be given a delicate and priceless antique from a museum and told that if it were unspoiled after a length of time you could keep it and have unlimited access to everything in the museum. How would this scenario change your life? What choices would you make differently?

We also have a treasure inside of us. Priceless and powerful. A treasure that grants us an audience with the Creator of the universe and access to the riches of heaven as family heirs. What is this treasure? None other than the Spirit of the Living God.

But just like a rebellious child, some of us have rejected being a part of the only family that will spend eternity with God. In some cases, we have acted like *trust-fund* kids and took for granted the riches of our inheritance in Christ and dirtied the family name with shameful behavior. Some even run away from their family, proud of the inheritance they have but ashamed to be associated with their siblings.

But when you carry this kind of treasure inside of you, you are called to something higher than your old ways of living. You become a representative, an ambassador, of what you carry. A human temple, walking to wherever you are directed and carrying the Creator to those He created so that they also can become what He created them for.

Take some time to evaluate what kind of a representative you have been. Do you live up to the family calling of your new family in Christ? Our Father is not looking for perfection, He knows our failings and weaknesses. What He is looking for is us being perfected in Him as we walk with Him. But while we walk, we must remember what we carry inside.

Notes:

_____

_____

_____

_____

_____

"If another believer sins against you, go privately and point out the offense. If the other person listens and confesses it, you have won that person back. But if you are unsuccessful, take one or two others with you and go back again, so that everything you say may be confirmed by two or three witnesses. If the person still refuses to listen, take your case to the church. Then if he or she won't accept the church's decision, treat that person as a pagan or a corrupt tax collector."

— *Matthew 18:15-17, NLT*

Some believe if their heart is right with their Father that is all that matters. But our Father says if your heart or actions aren't right with His other kids then they aren't right with Him either.

To come into the light is painful at first, and you will squint for a while until your eyes adjust. But when you become used to living in the light, you can operate without needing as many adjustments. It's much like keeping your brotherly relations up to date.

It is hard to sit down with someone and have hard conversations about wrong that is going on. Our Western thinking wants to squirm away in avoidance. It's uncomfortable. You might face rejection and scrutiny head-on at times. You may strengthen the friendship, or it may need to end. But the result of staying in the light is always worth it in the end.

You get one heart, and that heart is either blocked by sin or freed by grace. A heart blocked holds grudges, gives in to bitterness and thinks selfishly. But a heart freed by our Father's forgiveness can forgive. It releases old grudges and considers the needs of others.

People will stumble, and who on earth knows our faults better than our spiritual siblings? The decision is ours. Will we decide to work it out? Our Father, like a good father, tells us to go and first make things right with others (Matthew 5:23-24). Even if others don't come to us asking for forgiveness, or are penitent at all, the command is still to forgive and release them back into the hands of the Father who loves them just as much as He loves you.

Take some time to examine your heart. Is there a situation that needs to be brought up with another brother or sister in Christ? If there is, use wisdom and solid counsel. Be brave when the time is right to bring it up, and wise in the way that you bring it up. God wants His kids to be one; one in Him and one with each other.

Notes:

_____

_____

_____

_____

_____

"Do not abandon me, O Lord. Do not stand at a distance, my God. Come quickly to help me, O Lord my savior."

— *Psalm 38:21-22, NLT*

"The eyes of the Lord watch over those who do right; His ears are open to their cries for help."

— *Psalm 34:15, NLT*

One day, when my kids were very young, I took them to a street festival. It was crowded with people and attractions, and distractions were everywhere. As we walked along the street, I noticed my son had gotten distracted and wasn't following closely. I kept my eye on him but allowed him to slowly drift away from where my daughter and I were. Five feet. Ten feet. When we reached twenty feet apart, he realized I was not next to him. I saw the panic well up in his face as he frantically looked back and forth. Within seconds he began to cry, and I walked over to comfort him. Although he was never out of my sight, he had probably felt all alone.

So often in my life that little boy was me. Wondering where my Father was and realizing I had allowed myself to drift apart from Him. Many distractions in life had vied for my attention. And very often it wasn't a deliberate and rebellious act of leaving God, but the outcome was the same.

The first thing that goes when you allow yourself to drift away from your Father is the desire to spend time with Him. Devotions give way to one more tv show. Bible reading gets pushed aside for that exciting fiction book. And prayer time slowly gets replaced with time with friends or busyness. Most times it's innocent at first. But sometimes we forget that these distractions in excess are often the trailhead to a path that drifts us away from our Father.

Yesterday is gone; and tomorrow is a mystery. But if we decide now to return to our Father, then our *past* can truly be gone, *now* can be a joy, and our *future* will be filled with hope.

———————

Take some time to test your level of closeness with your Father. If you feel you have drifted off, don't wait until you are very far before course correcting. Little, intentional acts caused us to drift away. And it will be the little, intentional acts of reaching back to our Father that will build closeness again. Your Father has His eyes on you and always will. He displayed this by sending His best for our worst and reaches out for us to return to Him while there is time.

Notes:

_____

_____

_____

_____

_____

"Behold, I stand at the door and knock. If anyone hears My voice and opens the door, I will come in to him and dine with him, and he with Me."

— Revelation 3:20, NKJV

All throughout this passage is the pleading of One who loves calling to those who have forgotten that love. They were so content to go through the motions of their lives that the object of their worship was not welcomed in.

Have you been at this crossroad before? Coming to the realization that the God whom you worship has not been the god you've been serving? If you have, and you quieted yourself, did you feel the *gentle cords* (Hosea 11:4) seeking to draw you near again to the one and only source of life?

Jesus is calling us back to our first calling: to follow and be with Him. Where you spend your time will tell others what you care about more than your words. Because time is our costliest resource, and we guard it closely. If we allow access to our Father, He can bring us into our calling. But a closed off and guarded heart will keep Him outside knocking to get in.

He isn't forcing you to do anything. The choice to spend time with our Father must be ours. Just like every good father He doesn't want forced obedience; He wants willing obedience. A choice made by sons and daughters in love with their Father. And if we are willingly disobedient, we will find ourselves on the road to a destination we don't want to be at.

The road that Jesus uses to bring forgiveness must first be paved with repentance. We only have one heart and one door to our innermost being. Bitterness, anger, unforgiveness, laziness, apathy, jealousy, and pride are among the many things that can shut it. But repentance and healing are the way we open it back up.

Take some time to do an inventory of your heart. Are you making time to be with Him? Or are you mismanaging your 24 hours? Are you allowing room for Him, or do you crowd Him out with a full schedule? And if you find yourself on the road of disobedience, you don't have to continue down that path. You can repent, turn around, and begin anew with your Father.

Notes:

_____

_____

_____

_____

_____

"Why are you cast down, O my soul? And why are you disquieted within me? Hope in God, for I shall yet praise Him for the help of His countenance."

— Psalm 42:5, NKJV

My dad and I were exhausted after hiking most way up a trail one summer day. The finish line seemed to evade us with each ridge we crossed, and we were about ready to quit. Our words soon reflected our inner thoughts, and we considered turning around. But when we crossed the last ridge and saw the slope to the mountain camp, our hopes revived. My dad said, "It's right there!" We then changed our tone from defeat to victory and were able to push to the end.

Have you ever spoken negatively to yourself? Or to others? For most of us, the answer to both is a resounding yes. But the absence of negative words is not the goal. The goal is to become more like our Savior, who framed the world with His words, and whose fatherly thoughts toward us cannot be counted. That means our words and thoughts are the way we battle in the arena of the mind.

David was in a bit of a situation. One of many in his lifetime, and many of which were his own doing. But he made a choice when he felt crushed on the inside. Instead of giving in to his feelings and thoughts with his words, he chose to speak life into himself. Because David was a proficient warrior, he knew what led to defeat. A defeated spirit is a doorway that leads to many other defeats. It saps the life out of you, draining you of hope.

So where did David start? He started with honesty and addressed how he was feeling head on. But he didn't stay there for long, and instead of questioning God's motives, he put his own feelings on trial. Then he spoke truth over himself and pointed his focus back to his source of security.

We often need to be reminded of the truth, especially when we are discouraged. This requires your active participation, both in your mind and with your voice. Not every thought that enters your mind is yours. So be ready to *cast down* anything that doesn't lead you to follow and obey your Father.

―――――――

Take some time to reflect on what words you have been speaking over yourself and others. Have you used words of life, or of defeat and hopelessness? If words and thoughts of defeat have poured out of you, you have an opportunity today to turn the tide. Instead of negativity and lies, begin thinking and speaking the truth your Father speaks over you. Speak His words, and think His thoughts, until the life of His Son can be seen in you.

Notes:

_____

_____

_____

_____

_____

"Judge not, that you be not judged. For with what judgement you judge, you will be judged; and with the measure you use, it will be measured back to you. And why do you look at the speck in your brother's eye, but do not consider the plank in your own eye? Or how can you say to your brother, 'Let me remove the speck from your eye', and look, a plank is in your own eye? Hypocrite! First remove the plank from your own eye, and then you will see clearly to remove the speck from your brother's eye."

— Matthew 7:1-5, NKJV

You can't help others effectively unless you've gone through a process of healing, repentance, and growth. Notice God didn't say to never help others who have failings. Or to not recognize when someone has an area needing growth. What He is saying is things must be set right in you first before you can help others see their faults. That process helps give you the right heart and approach to help others.

God's intent is for His people to reach out their hands and hearts to help those around them. But a refining process is necessary to keep our heart aligned with God's heart for others.

People with scars may have stories, but only people with scars who carry the life and joy of Christ inside have the story people need to hear to have healing themselves. A story of how God brought healing and can do it again and again! They have received from the heart of God and now understand how to reach others who are walking through the same process.

It often takes those who have been broken to know how to approach those who are broken. It takes someone who has walked through repentance to know how to approach those still living a life of sin. It takes someone with healed scars to know how to approach those who are still wounded.

Too many read verses 1 to 4 and completely ignore verse 5, the verse that displays God's heart and main objective. God wants His lost, broken, and rebellious kids brought back into the family! And how does God want to do this? By using His hands and feet; by using us!

Our Father can at times supernaturally use us to offer what we don't have. But more often, we can't bring anything to anyone except what we already have inside. If you carry a heart healed and forgiven from your past, then God can absolutely use you if you are willing. But the best thing we can both carry and give to others is the love and forgiveness we also have received freely from our Father.

—————

Take some time to examine your inner life. What areas have you been healed, forgiven, or set free from? How can you allow God to use you to help others who are going through a similar process? Also, what areas do you still need healing? Forgiveness? Growth? If you have sin, confess it. If you have wounds, lay it open to God, the Master Surgeon. If you need to grow in an area, then stay around a quality community of believers who have grown in that area.

Notes:

_____

_____

_____

_____

_____

"Then hear from heaven Your dwelling place, and forgive, and give to everyone according to all his ways, whose heart You know (for You alone know the hearts of the sons of men), that they may fear You, to walk in Your ways as long as they live in the land which You gave to our fathers."

— 2 Chronicles 6:30-31, NKJV

"Imitate me, just as I also imitate Christ."

— 1 Corinthians 11:1, NKJV

A good leader will always point you to something greater. That's because a good leader must first be a good follower. One who has practiced the art of listening and applying changes to their lives.

Always point people back to their true source: their Father. How limiting it would be if my source were a pastor, teacher, business leader, or political figure. They could only give me what they have. We all need examples to follow in our lives, and some may be positive, although limited.

But how freeing would it make a person when they receive directly from the Creator of the universe! The One who knows every aspect of our being, fashioned out our gifting and talents before we were born, sees our inadequacies and yet still loves us with a love we can't begin to fathom.

Never substitute your time with your Father with the voice or time of someone lesser. Even a devotional, however helpful it may be, should never take the place of your audience with the King.

If someone comes to you needing advice, do you also encourage them to ask their Father about it? If not, even if your advice is good, it could rob them of the opportunity to hear and be led directly from their true source. Our heart should always be in a posture to seek the best for those around us. But if we don't also point them back to their Father, we may unwittingly show our inner belief that our advice is better than God's guidance.

Take some time to ask your Father how you can point those around you back to Him more. We all need encouraging relationships in our lives and building them is effort well spent. But in addition to being a source of encouragement and advice, develop a habit of having a heart that says: "I'll give you what I have, but hear from God as well and listen to Him first." This is a form of worship. Displaying our belief that God gives the best advice. Of releasing our control over others and trusting Him to guide them.

Notes:

_____

_____

_____

_____

_____

"O Lord, why do You stand so far away? Why do You hide when I am in trouble?"

— Psalm 10:1, NLT

God is not afraid of *why* questions. You can pour out your heart to Him and ask all the tough questions you want. He has big shoulders and can handle them. Maybe you have been through rough situations or struggles. You might ask, 'Why did You let this happen?' Or vent to Him, 'I don't understand this, God!'

He isn't afraid of what you might say. Like a parent who knows how to read the face of their children, He already knows what is on your heart anyway.

When David cried out to God, he really dug deep and didn't hold back. He held no shame in telling God he felt lost and hurt. He frequently lamented that he felt abandoned and wounded by others. But he always came back to who he knew God to be, and never called God's character into question.

That wholehearted trust in who David knew God to be, despite the pain and struggles David went through, led him to a place of healing. There was still a big gap between the questions and who he knew God was. But instead of clinging to the questions, he anchored to the truth. He opened himself up to his Father, exposing his pain, anxiety, and confusion.

Whatever we go through, God's character doesn't change. He isn't different because we go through pain, or when situations don't make sense. He is still the Father of love who wants more than anything for you to lean on Him.

We live in a fallen world, with fallen people who will do what fallen people do. We won't always know *why*; sometimes there won't be a *why*. But there is a Father who will never change, and we can know Him. He is waiting to hear from you.

Take some time alone to dig deep and ask your Father your hard questions. And after you do, remind yourself of who your Father is and His character. Let your anchor, your foundation, be who God says He is. He won't change. He won't abandon you. And when life doesn't make sense, it's the character of God that you can lean on to see you through.

Notes:

_____

_____

_____

_____

_____

"He who dwells in the secret place of the Most High shall abide under the shadow of the Almighty."

— Psalm 91:1, NKJV

"But you, when you pray, go into your room, and when you have shut your door, pray to your Father who is in the secret place; and your Father who sees in secret will reward you openly."

— Matthew 6:6, NKJV

Have you ever wanted advice from the smartest people in the world? Or be able to listen to high level conversations from world leaders? Or at the very least hang around with the most influential people?

There is something special about getting insider knowledge or being able to rub shoulders with the upper echelons of society. It gives you a sense of importance to be included. To one level or another we all want to be included, invited, and to have access to areas we consider important.

Moses knew this firsthand. He was invited by God to join in with His plans. To take council and confer directly with Him. To hear His voice and His thoughts. To meet with Him face to face. And from that place of meeting, Moses was able to take what he had learned and use it to influence others.

What you do in secret will affect how you live in the open. What you marinate in at home is the flavor you will carry when you leave. Like any aroma it will be evident to those around you.

When you spend time in secret with your Father, you can boldly walk in public. And the more time you spend, the more His scent rubs off on you. How you speak begins to sound more and more like how He speaks. Your decisions begin to line up with His. And as your ways transform, you begin to walk in the blessing of your Father.

Take some time to get away so you can be alone with God. But don't let your time with Him be limited to the usual. Focus on quality, even if all you have is fifteen minutes. Let that time, however long it is, be the spark to light the incense you will carry with you.

Notes:

_____

_____

_____

_____

_____

"And you must commit yourselves wholeheartedly to these commands that I am giving you today. Repeat them again and again to your children. Talk about them when you are at home and when you are on the road, when you are going to bed and when you are getting up. Tie them to your hands and wear them on your forehead as reminders. Write them on the doorpost of your house and on your gates."

— Deuteronomy 6:6-9, NLT

While walking along the river's edge I stopped and admired the flowing sounds of water. The light gurgling and splashing sounds soothed the atmosphere all around. Almost unnoticed in the peaceful scene was the important work going on non-stop below the surface. But staring at the meandering current confirmed a truth: there were no sharp rocks in the river.

In life we are very much like the rock. We are shaped by what we allow into our lives. We can go with the flow and conform to the current of this world. But if we stay in the stream of our Father's words, He can shape us into the image of His Son.

Just like rocks need the steady flow of the water to be polished with sand and sediment, so the truths of your Fathers words carry life that will shape you. But only if you let it consistently flow over and through you. The truths, challenges, and corrections will act like grit, sanding away at the edges.

We are all prone to forget. And what is unused will slowly fade and be lost. That is why we need to hear the truth again and again. It is why we need to put into practice kindness and hospitality. It is why we need to exercise our faith by taking steps toward where our Father leads.

What will you allow to be the water? Are you being shaped more by God's word and truths, or the world system? You may have come to your Father like a sharp and jagged rock. But time in the river of His words can smooth your edges until you are made new.

———————

Take some time to evaluate what you are being shaped and influenced by. If negative forces or even people are controlling the thermostat of your actions, attitudes, or spiritual life, instead of what comes from your Father, then commit today to a reset. Set your thoughts, words, and actions on what your Father says. Repeat them over and over. Make it an anthem continually over your life. Then, little by little, you will be shaped to look more like a son or daughter of the King.

Notes:

_____

_____

_____

_____

_____

*"If we confess our sins, He is faithful and just to forgive us
our sins and to cleanse us from all unrighteousness."*

– 1 John 1:9, NKJV

*"Restore to me the joy of Your salvation, and
uphold me by Your generous Spirit."*

– Psalm 51:12, NKJV

Are you happy to be forgiven from your sin, or still full of guilt that you sinned? To those burdened by their past sins and failures, guilt and shame are familiar traveling companions. Often our sins stare us down and remind us of the past (Psalm 51:3). Even after we repent, we sometimes carry the sting of *the past* long after the time when it was *the present*.

But there is a healing that comes with walking in the light (1 John 1:7). Our failures cause us to want to alienate from other believers. Exposing our sins to the light of Christ causes us to have restored relationships and fellowship.

Where pride destroyed, newfound humility can slowly help build. Where anger separated, the love of Christ in our hearts draws others together. Where bitterness and envy festered sores on our souls, forgiveness can put on the healing ointment.

When we confess our sins and choose to walk in openness and transparency with our hearts, minds and actions then broken things can be fixed. But these actions must be walked out.

There is healing in the *walking out* process. Yes, our sins have been washed, but our minds like to hold onto our old stuff. It is during *the walking* that our condemnation can also be healed (Romans 8:1).

Remember, failure doesn't have to be fatal, because God is faithful.

Take time to ask God what areas of your life need to be exposed to the light. Confess them and bring them to Him. Then target those areas of sin, or old wounds, that have kept you from fellowship with other believers. Begin living out Christlike and Spirit led actions in the light of Christ to restore those relationships and to build new ones.

Notes:

_____

_____

_____

_____

_____

"Now it was in the heart of my father David to build a temple for the name of the Lord God of Israel. But the Lord said to my father David, 'Whereas it was in your heart to build a temple for My name, you did well in that it was in your heart. Nevertheless you shall not build the temple, but your son who will come from your body, he shall build the temple for My name.'"

— 2 Chronicles 6:7-9, NKJV

It's not your job to do everything. To be everything. To accomplish everything. Even if at times you feel you really want to.

Sometimes we get so focused on what we need to do to build our lives or ministries that we miss out on the most important building process of all: building into the next generation.

David took great care to pour into Solomon as a father. Although not always perfect, he set Solomon up for success with training, instruction, provisions he would need, and a deep desire for wisdom. As a result, Solomon was able to make his father's floor his ceiling and walk into his purpose.

We often only think a few steps ahead. We plan and strategize days, weeks, and maybe years into the future. But God thinks generationally and sees how your piece of the puzzle connects to the next generation's piece, and the next and so on.

There is power in passing on the torch so others can run with it. But before we can do that, we must prepare others to run with it. David did this by instructing Solomon on how a king should reign and even prepared him for some of the struggles he would soon face. You could say David helped build the man who would later be able to build God's temple.

Who are you building? Is there anyone who is receiving instruction or advice from you on what God has done in your life?

Your life lessons were not meant for you alone, but as a blessing to change your circle of influence and beyond. It may feel intimidating at first, just as many things are when you first try. Ask God to show you this week who you can begin pouring into and what words you can speak. And if you need wisdom, God loves to give it if we are open enough to ask!

Notes:

_____

_____

_____

_____

_____

"Your word is a lamp to guide my feet and a light for my path."

— Psalm 119:105, NLT

"The law of his God is in his heart; none of his steps shall slide."

— Psalm 37:31, NKJV

A map may guide you to your destination; but a light will help you get there safely. No amount of direction will help if you can't see around you. The rocks might trip you, or you might step into a hole. And even if you manage to feel and stumble your way in the dark, think of all the trouble you could have avoided by walking with a light.

It's the same with our Father's Word. It doesn't tell us what vocation we should go into, or where to live, or who we will marry. Instead, it shows us what work ethic to carry into our callings, how to live wherever we are, and how to show love and raise a family. It can show you potential danger and alert you to things hidden. With His Word He helps us walk confidently in a world full of darkness.

When you receive direction from God's Spirit, our Father's Word helps us carry that vision with integrity. We need both God's Word and the voice of His Spirit. If His book showed us everything in our future, why would we ever need to trust Him for what's next? Our Father gives us the light of His Word to help walk out the steps we get by listening to His voice. And only when we take those steps will we see the ones that come after.

Just like a lamp will cast its light only a few steps ahead, so God's Words offers us illumination in our situation. The future may still be a mystery, but with our Father's light we won't face that mystery in the dark.

Take some time to think through what situations you are in that need some light. Ask your Father for wisdom from His book to help you. Then begin digging in. Meditate on what you read. Commentaries and word searches can also be helpful if we don't use them as a substitute for reading His word for ourselves.

Notes:

_____

_____

_____

_____

_____

"The end of all things is near; therefore, be of sound judgement and sober spirit for the purpose of prayer."

– 1 Peter 4:7, NASB

Do you feel your words aren't important? Or that prayer is a casual exercise to use only when most convenient?

We often forget that words from the mouth of the Master Creator Himself formed the oceans, mountains, sun, and stars. We forget that words brought everything into existence. With a pure focus and clear vision words sparked life where there was none. Because He had not only the authority, but the desire, to do so.

Is your vision clear and your mind set on your calling to pray? We have all been given areas of influence that we can speak into. We all have opportunities to stand in the gap and cry out to God on behalf of our families, communities, and country. But will we use our God-given authority as sons and daughters, and ambassadors of God's coming government?

When we are undistracted of the worries around us and carry a sober spirit that hears from God, we can more accurately target prayer needs. If we carry the heart of the Master Creator, then our spirit can be filled with the burden of God's focus. And when we focus and target in prayer what God has purposed in His heart, we can know our prayers are directed correctly.

But how can we do this until we spiritually *sober-up* to one of our most important callings? We must have the sound judgement to set aside distractions and purpose our lives to be about God's governmental business of prayer and intercession.

Take some time in your personal time to pray. Ask your Father to show you more about your calling to pray. Your words have power. The Father Who adopted you into His family is calling you to do what He first did: to speak and watch things come to life. So let your words mirror His will and watch that prayer partnership create new life.

Notes:

_____

_____

_____

_____

_____

"'I've obeyed all these commandments,' the young man replied. 'What else must I do?' Jesus told him, 'If you want to be perfect, go and sell all your possessions and give the money to the poor, and you will have treasure in heaven. Then come, follow me.' But when the young man heard this, he went away sad, for he had many possessions."

— Matthew 19:20-22, NLT

Jesus exposed the one area that wasn't fully surrendered. Wealth and possessions had become a *god* and source for this man instead of relying on his Father. The man was willing to jump through hoops, obey a bunch of rules, humble himself for advice, serve or do whatever he could do to get on God's good side.

But wealth, power, and *things* had become an idol deep in his heart, and his heart couldn't serve two masters.

Jesus wasted no time granting his wish and pointed out the right path to hike. He showed him the only way to get to heaven to be with his Father was through Jesus; to follow Him in obedience. But giving up the control he had as a wealthy person of status was a cost he was unwilling to pay. Jesus gave him the answer, and he didn't like it.

We often pray to our Father for answers, all the while having what we believe should be His response. But when our Father gives us an answer, and we don't like it, what should we do? Do we allow ourselves to be hurt and offended by the only One who has the answers we need?

Obedience is a test not only of our trust in our Father but also of love. Because love shows itself, it cannot hide for long. The young man's trust and love was in his wealth, and his heart resisted choosing what was contrary to his primary love.

Take some time to examine the source of your trust and love. Imagine what could get stripped away, and what you could not allow to leave your life. What would it look like if all your money, prestige, or honor was stripped away? When confronted with the choice would you be ready to decide?

Life will test this. But allowing yourself to evaluate your heart beforehand is a good step. When your love and trust are in Him, although apprehensive and scared, you can follow Him into the dark unknown of any forest when He says: "Follow Me."

Notes:

_____

_____

_____

_____

_____

*"Fathers, do not provoke your children to anger by the way
you treat them. Rather, bring them up with the discipline
and instruction that comes from the Lord."*

– Ephesians 6:4, NLT

After I had yelled at my child for doing wrong, I, like many parents, stomped off and asked God for wisdom in dealing with the problems that arise. I love asking God for wisdom because He gives it generously. The challenging part is His wisdom often involves us doing things we don't want to do or growing in ways we think we are not ready to grow.

After I waited a while, I heard Him speak softly, but so firmly it knocked the wind out of my sails. A question of few words, but deep with meaning. Subtle, yet the point was clear. Because His questions are packed with answers.

He asked: *Have I ever yelled at you?*

Have you ever heard God yell at you? I've heard others yell at me. I've even yelled at myself from time to time. But I've never heard God yell at me, or even barely raise His voice. And yet He gets to the heart of every one of my issues with just a few soft words.

Contrast this with Psalm 29 which displays the power and authority of God's voice. It is true that God's voice is powerful, intricate, and precise; but it can also be delicate. The voice of our Creator is just as powerful when He whispers in our hearts as when His voice thunders in the heavens. Because God knows how to speak in different circumstances.

The problem is we get good at crowding out His voice. We get busy. We don't sit still long enough to hear the lovingly corrective voice of our Father. I've often heard people say, "if God wants my attention, He knows how to get it." But I wonder how many of us are willing to give our attention to Him in the first place.

Look back at your life. Was it the harshness of God or His kindness that led you to turn from your old life to be made new? Did He practice patience with you or expect you to get it right the first time?

If I'm not in love enough with my Father that I would strain to hear His whisper, why would I think Him yelling at me would bring about my obedience?

———————

Take some time to think about how you have used your words with those around you. If your words are not full of the fruit of the Spirit, then it is time to transform. This will involve putting new things in your mind constantly until old ways are washed out. But use God's words because His words are best for ridding yourself of your old ways and forming new ways.

Notes:

_____

_____

_____

_____

_____

"And when the Pharisees saw it, they said to His disciples, 'Why does your Teacher eat with tax collectors and sinners?' When Jesus heard that, He said to them, 'Those who are well have no need of a physician, but those who are sick. But go and learn what this means: "I desire mercy and not sacrifice." For I did not come to call the righteous, but sinners, to repentance.'"

— Matthew 9:11-13, NKJV

What God wants to see done in the earth is for those who carry His heart to reflect who He is so others can carry His heart also.

God has none above Him to reach to, or anyone equal, so all He can do is reach down to us. And He loves it when we reach back up to Him, just like children wanting to be held. And just like children, He pulls us close and shows us what He is really like.

But when He looks down and sees those hurting around us His greatest desire is to pull them close also. And because He is a good Father, He teaches His children to be a part of His work.

But instead of pulling people to us, we as the hands and feet of our Brother Jesus are to help them by putting their hands into His. It's our greatest mission: to point people to the One who wants them back desperately.

We do have a part to play. We can help with practical things, but we can never give true peace. We can be there to talk, cry, and be a presence, but we can never give healing. Those are things only God can do. We have our part, and God has His. And being able to work with Him is the best family business anyone could ever be in.

Take some time to think of who you can show the love of Jesus to. The kind of love that goes to where people are at, and without compromise displays a purity and love they never knew existed. Ask God how you can be used this week to be like your Father, who desperately wants to pull others back up to Him.

Notes:

_____

_____

_____

_____

_____

"A third time He asked him, 'Simon son of John, do you love Me?' Peter was hurt that Jesus asked the question a third time. He said, 'Lord, you know everything. You know that I love You.' Jesus said, 'Then feed My sheep.'"

– John 21:17, NLT

One time, when I had once again sinned against my Father, I spent some time in silence and felt Him ask: "Why don't you love Me?" The question hit me to the core. Why would He ask me that? Of course I loved Him. Or did I?

Even from the beginning our Father wanted our love first and foremost. Because when He had our unconditional love, obedience would easily flow from our committed hearts. But often, our obedience only reaches to the level of our love. And just like the Israelites in the wilderness our Father is asking for us to love Him.

I've heard it said before that love is a verb. It shows itself both through what we do and don't do. Our love shows itself in where we put our time, effort, and energy. It is not confined to the box of our feelings but gives all in the arena of our lives. It can be fostered to grow or neglected to fade away. And with each day, hour, or minute, it all begins with a choice.

Love can be something living and breathing in our lives. But to have it we must first make a choice and continually put that choice into action. Every time we make a choice to love, we show outwardly what we have chosen inwardly. Even inaction is a choice.

Our Father, long ago, gave us an example by making a choice and putting it into action. From near the beginning of the story until now, our mountain of failings caused us to have a just penalty of spiritual death; us as children eternally separated from a loving Father. Only a high price, the perfect sacrifice, would bring true justice for all our crimes. Not wanting to spend eternity away from us, the love in His heart compelled our Father to action. He sent His very best, His only Son, to take the punishment on Himself so that if we choose to be one with His Son, we can be adopted back into the family. But the choice is ours.

Take some time to examine where your heart is towards your Father. What do your actions or inactions show about how much or little you love Him? We all stumble in different areas at times. These moments show our need to be perfected and to grow in His love. If we allow these moments to be teachable ones, then our love can be deepened. And we can realize how vast our Father's love is for us. He already gave His all and keeps giving out of the abundance of His love. The question is: will we choose to love Him in return?

Notes:

_____

_____

_____

_____

_____

*"But the end of all things is at hand, therefore be
serious and watchful in your prayers."*

— 1 Peter 4:7, NKJV

*"Confess your trespasses to one another, and pray for one another, that you
may be healed. The effective, fervent prayer of a righteous man avails much."*

— James 5:16, NKJV

Do you go to work only when you feel like it? Do you love and respect your spouse and kids only when you feel in the mood? Do you do good only when it is convenient?

It is easy to love, give, and respect when it is out of a response to something given to us. But to do these things before receiving can take faith, and a whole lot of guts.

It takes faith to sow into prayer. Prayer is an investment into what is often not seen. It can be a response when we feel God's presence strongly and prayer seems to spring from our inner core. But at other times it feels like hiking up a steep hill when we are already tired.

We must remember that prayer is both a destination and a journey, much like communication in marriage. Most people can communicate a thought or idea to someone else. But to build up the trust and deep connection from a lifetime of solid communication is a journey, and to get there takes time.

If you haven't begun this journey, or have gone off the trail, there is good news: you can begin right where you are at! Jesus told us to ask of His Father. From asking for forgiveness to become a part of His family, to asking what we have need of, to asking for our family, community, and nation.

Take some time to get on your knees in whatever capacity you can and begin the journey of consistent communication with a Father who loves you. Thank Him for things, praise Him for things, just get to talking. Break the wall of passive silence and practice intentionality. Some days will feel like a downhill trek with a cool breeze, others might feel like sludging uphill in the rain. Just don't get hung up on how you feel. Because the most important, most influential, most powerful Person in the universe is asking you to come talk with Him. So, talk.

Notes:

_____

_____

_____

_____

_____

"Let the words of my mouth and the meditation of my heart be acceptable in Your sight, O Lord, my strength and my Redeemer."

— Psalm 19:14, NKJV

The words we speak come from our heart (Matthew 15:18). Those words affect our habits, our habits help shape our beliefs, and our core beliefs steer our heart. It can be a vicious or life-giving cycle, depending on our focus. Every part of the cycle can be affected by the others. Once put on the right track, it is a life-giving loop. But taken off course it becomes a train wreck.

But you are not a victim of this cycle. Instead, you are its cultivator.

You have been given something nothing else in creation has: a soul with a will. You can choose life or death. Healthy or unhealthy. You have been given a mind and are in control over what you put into it. But we must understand that every part of us is connected.

You may be able to fake it for a time, but what is in your heart will come out. If something wrong comes out, we are tempted to ask ourselves: "why did I say that?" The question we should ask instead is: "what have I been filling my heart with?"

Don't follow your heart. In its unrenewed state it is extremely deceptive. It seldom gives good advice and instead selfishly looks to its own pleasure. Your words are not far behind, and both need to be tamed (James 3:1-12).

Just like the captain of a ship, you use your *rudder* by making a choice. A choice of what to say, do, or think. A choice of what you will watch and how you will spend your time. A choice to submit yourself to your Father's ways, or your own.

Wanting your heart and mind to be purified and renewed, all the while filling it with thoughts, words, and entertainment that are impure, is like wishing to be healthy but eating a garbage diet. You are what you eat, and what you think and speak (Proverbs 23:7)

———————

Take some time to evaluate what has been coming out of your heart. Your heart and words are like gauges, showing the condition of what is inside. If what you see coming out does not reflect the heart of your Father, then today you can make a different choice. That is what true repentance is; a humbling of yourself and choosing to follow the right path once again.

Notes:

_____

_____

_____

_____

_____

"But new wine must be put into new wineskins, and both are preserved."

— Luke 5:38, NKJV

What are some of the changes God is working into your life? What new adventures do you believe God is drawing you into? Do you believe they are connected?

We often yearn for the day when God brings us into the future He has for us. But sometimes, we neglect the process of change and refinement we must go through to get there. This is true from the little things to the big things.

Do you want to have a family? Then how are you preparing yourself to be a part of that family? Do you want a better job? Then how are you growing and learning to be able to function in that job? What kind of service has God called you to? In what ways can you be faithful to prepare you to serve others in that capacity?

Our impact on others has far more to do with who we are than what we do. That is why God works change on the inside before we see anything else on the outside.

But change requires action steps. Steps like forgiving others and asking forgiveness, practicing humility, and removing unhealthy practices from our lives. God can pinpoint what needs to change, but we also can proactively do inventory of what needs to change.

But while taking all the practical, sacrificial steps, let's not forget to tune our ears to God's voice. Because obedience is by far the most important step.

Take some time to both remember and listen. Remember what God has spoken to you and listen to what He is speaking to you and begin walking that out. But also find practical steps that you can take to grow and mature. Our Father will do His part; will we do ours?

Notes:

_____

_____

_____

_____

_____

"And let us consider one another in order to stir up love and good works, not forsaking the assembling of ourselves together, as is the manner of some, but exhorting one another, and so much the more as you see the Day approaching."

— Hebrews 10:24-25, NKJV

Have you ever given up on meeting with your brothers and sisters in Christ? Have wounds, fear, or other insecurities driven you away from those who you've been called to build up? It's time to remember the part you are supposed to play.

An orchestra is made up of dozens of musicians each playing their own instrument as part of a whole. Each of them is tasked with practicing their own instrument, both by themselves and with the team. Each part may sound good but is incomplete by itself. And when the time comes to perform together each helps keep their fellow musicians on track. If one of them makes a mistake, others can help that one to merge back in with the group.

A musician may get better by themselves but will never reach their full potential without other quality musicians. There is something special when a group of musicians can operate as a single unit making one sound while using multiple instruments.

We as believers are being built together as a dwelling place for God (Ephesians 2:22). Like a musician in an orchestra, you are a part of something greater. You are called to strengthen and build up those around you, and they likewise for you. Some have been wounded while trying to be part of that family orchestra, showing that there is a lot of growth we all can benefit from.

Has something caused you to put down your *instrument*, or walk away from your family orchestra and try at it alone? If this is you, please know that God can heal an old wound. Let God bring healing with whatever went down and let Him show you where you can be a part of the team again.

We all need growth and are at different places in our journeys. But the sound that is produced from a team that has one purpose and focus is unsurpassed.

Take some time to look through areas of hurt that have caused you to withdraw from other believers. Ask God to show them to you. Once He has shown you, ask your Father to give you steps of healing. This might include counseling, but usually includes large doses of forgiveness and humility.

Ask God what group of believers He wants you to partner with for this season. Remember that you have a part to play in building others up using the gifts God has given you. And if you don't know how, God can give wisdom to grow in your gifts so you can help build others up.

Notes:

_____

_____

_____

_____

_____

"And having a High Priest over the house of God, let us draw near with a true heart in full assurance of faith, having our hearts sprinkled from an evil conscience and our bodies washed with pure water. Let us hold fast the confession of our hope without wavering, for He who promised is faithful."

– Hebrews 10:21-23, NKJV

Have you ever been a faker? Have you ever felt you had to keep up appearances around your spiritual brothers and sisters?

When suiting up for a hike at the trailhead it is easy to tell the difference between someone who knows what they are doing and those who don't. From putting on gear to small trail courtesies, all reveal their experience level. We all were once beginners. And the choice all beginners have is to either fake it, or to be brave enough to watch, learn, and ask questions.

God wants us to come to Him boldly with a true heart, just like a son or daughter would. He also wants us to function well together as a family. The problem is if we are carrying insecurities, wounds, or fears that aren't healed, we might be tempted to throw on a smile and feign confidence.

So instead of drawing near to God or others with a true heart, we put on our fake face. The problem with doing that is we block ourselves off from the life-giving areas that can bring healing. First the source of your Father, then family, solid community, quality counsel, and godly friendships.

The choice is yours. Will you fake it? Or are you willing to live in the light? Your Father isn't afraid of where you are, or your questions. And He's willing to walk with you because He is faithful.

———————————

Take some time to examine your heart for any areas you may be *wearing a mask*. Your Father wants you to come as you are with a true heart. And to be part of the family of believers. Past hurts may tempt us to fake, or forsake when it comes to our Father's family. Find solid brothers and sisters who are willing to walk with you. I've needed a few myself, and they are out there.

If you are willing to come to your Father with a true heart, hot mess and all, He will accept you. And don't worry about being perfect, either. Just be perfectly His and tell your fear to kick rocks.

Notes:

_____

_____

_____

_____

_____

*"Therefore the king said to me, 'Why is your face sad, since you are not
sick? This is nothing but sorrow of heart.' So I became dreadfully afraid,
and said to the king, 'May the king live forever! Why should my face not be
sad, when the city, the place of my fathers' tombs, lies waste, and its gates
are burned with fire?' Then the king said to me, 'What do you request?'
So I prayed to the God of heaven. And I said to the king, 'If it pleases the
king, and if your servant has found favor in your sight, I ask that you send
me to Judah, to the city of my fathers' tombs, that I may rebuild it.'"*

– Nehemiah 2:2-5, NKJV

Are you ready to ask for what God is brewing in your heart? Are
you ready for a blank check when you find your passion? Do you have
action steps to walk out what your Father is showing you in your area
of influence?

We are often better at answering questions about our purpose
within the confines of a box. But if someone asks you what your dream
is, are you ready to answer? And even more, are you ready to ask for
what you need to bring it into reality?

Nehemiah heard a report about the state of Jerusalem, and it rocked
him to the core. An irritation was growing inside him. A passion to
see something change. He couldn't shake the feeling of responsibility.
Deep down, an ownership of the problem was brewing. The irritation
pulled at him until he was faced with a choice.

That was the moment when his purpose touched the problem.

Nehemiah had lots of excuses for why he couldn't be the one to
solve that problem; he just didn't employ any of them. He instead
allowed himself the time to think, grieve, and pray until God's purpose
fully matured in his soul. And when asked by the king, Nehemiah laid
the situation out.

Because a passion had birthed in him, he was uniquely qualified to give voice to the situation. And when asked by the king what he needed to make it happen, he was prepared. He was prepared, because instead of wallowing in the problem, he marinated in the solution God wanted to bring to the problem and was ready to walk out his purpose by doing his part.

Take some time and ask your Father to begin birthing purpose in you. This can often be a process with many growth steps to prepare you. Be faithful with each one. And anytime a problem begins calling to the purpose inside of you, allow yourself the time so God can begin birthing a solution through you. It is a partnership we cannot accomplish much without, so allow your Father to use those *irritants* to refine the *pearl* inside you. Once it matures, your Father's mission can birth through you to the Earth He wants to reach.

Notes:

_____

_____

_____

_____

_____

"I know all the things you do. I have seen your hard work and your patient endurance. I know you don't tolerate evil people. You have examined the claims of those who say they are apostles but are not. You have discovered they are liars. You have patiently suffered for me without quitting. But I have this complaint against you. You don't love me or each other as you did at first! Look how far you have fallen! Turn back to me and do the works you did at first."

– Revelation 2:2-5a, NLT

As I descended a snow-covered mountain one foggy day, I began to get off track. I followed footprints in the snow that led me off course down a steep slope that I couldn't see the bottom of. I had lost my sense of direction in the blinding fog and became increasingly afraid of slipping down a slope into a crevasse. I finally decided to go back, retrace my steps, and find the correct path.

Have you made an idol of your service to God? Have you gotten to the point on your journey that following a set of rules replaces obedience to the One who gave those rules?

We all will worship something, whether we choose it or not. It is how we were built. When pushed, we all will decide on the number one in our lives. And out of countless possibilities, only one can have first place.

But what happens in the fog of life when we elevate the ways of God above God Himself? When we don't listen to the Spirit's voice in our heart, but are quick to enforce Christian values? Even rules can become an idol. And when following the path of rules instead of the loving God who made them, then like the church of Ephesus we might have left our first love.

Our Father must be our number one. And everything else, no matter how good, must take a lesser place. But how do we return? How do we get back on the right path after getting so lost in following the rules, instead of the Giver of all good things? We must retrace our steps.

Take some time to rekindle the passion you had when you first knew you were rescued from being eternally lost. Get your thankfulness on for everything your Father has given you because you are now His son or daughter. Go back to the simplicity that you first had, like a child gazing starry eyed into the eyes of the Father. Increasing in good works is both noble and necessary. But if we lose sight of our *first love,* we are lost in the *fog.*

Notes:

_____

_____

_____

_____

_____

"Next to them Jedaiah the son of Harumaph made repairs in front of his house. And next to him Hattush the son of Hashabniah made repairs."

— Nehemiah 3:10, NKJV

Everyone in Nehemiah who helped to build the wall of Jerusalem did so side by side with their neighbors, and most near where they lived. They weren't responsible for the whole city, just a small portion. Just like them, we may not be responsible for everything. But we are at least responsible for what is around us and what has been entrusted to us.

Sometimes we can't see the forest because of the trees. But, at other times, we often can't see the individual trees because the forest seems so vast. The *problems* seem so big we often miss our small part in the *solution*.

But we can't do it alone. We may have ownership in our *small part,* but we can't forget it will still take shoulder to shoulder work. Whether it is encouraging someone to continue strong in a broader scope of work or a smaller one, we each need encouragement to keep motivated.

One small gap in the wall can cause problems. One families unresolved problems can affect the neighborhood. One neighborhoods problems can affect the city. And one cities problems can weigh down a state and nation.

But just as light pushes out darkness, one fixed gap can mend problems. The light we carry as ambassadors of our Father with our words, actions, and prayers can change a family. One healed family can bring light to a whole neighborhood. One redeemed neighborhood can shine bright into the affairs of a city. And a city restored to the light of Christ can be a beacon of change and healing to a nation.

Take some time to reflect on your *section of the wall*. Just for a minute, ignore all the problems in the world and focus on the mission your Father is putting in front of you. Your gifting may be one indicator of your *section*, or your current situation, neighbors, or life trajectory. Look for the good that is in front of you to do, but also keep your focus on point to the mission that your Father has for you.

Notes:

_____

_____

_____

_____

_____

"As Jesus and the disciples approached Jerusalem, they came to the town of Bethphage on the Mount of Olives. Jesus sent two of them on ahead. 'Go into the village over there,' he said. 'As soon as you enter it, you will see a donkey tied there, with its colt beside it. Untie them and bring them to me. If anyone asks what you are doing, just say, "The Lord needs them," and he will immediately let you take them.'"

– Matthew 21:1-3, NLT

Does God really need us? He is God, right? Couldn't He use anything or anyone?

When the doubts come, and our inadequacies seem like a wall, it can be hard to believe that God would want to use us to do anything. But it is important when we begin feeling this way to remind ourselves that God wants us. Not only does He want us, He crafted you for an intended purpose.

The donkey and her colt He chose to fulfill the prophecy in Zechariah 9:9. But what an awesome picture of how God uses each of us. He knows us beforehand, and even sends people to us to be an influence. His desire is that we be untied from what bound us before and brought to Him. And as an instrument of Jesus, we too can carry Him into the places He wants to go. We also can be used by God. We also can fulfill our Father's purpose in the earth.

How very much like our Father to send His children to untie others along the way so they too can become part of His family. How very much like a good Father for Him to include us, when He really doesn't need us. But He chooses to partner with us for His purposes.

Most any father or mother knows they don't need their children to do much. And often it would be better and faster if we did it all ourselves. But a good parent knows to include their children in what they do so they will learn how to do it also.

It's the same way with our heavenly Father. He has a spot for us in the family business. He wants you to be His partner in His dealings and know what His plans are in His Kingdom. He wants to train you for what is ahead in the unique giftings He has given you. The question is, will you allow Him to?

Take some time to search if there are any areas you need to be untied from. Is anything holding you back from carrying Jesus into every area of your life? If there is, confess it, repent of it, whatever it is, and get free. Your Father is ready to teach you your purpose in His Kingdom, but we must put ourselves in a position of readiness to learn. Then we too can carry Jesus for His purpose.

Notes:

_____

_____

_____

_____

_____

"Beloved, do not think it strange concerning the fiery trial which is to try you, as though some strange thing happened to you; but rejoice to the extent that you partake of Christ's sufferings, that when His glory is revealed, you may also be glad with exceeding joy."

– 1 Peter 4:12-13, NKJV

God doesn't want us to be comfortable; He wants us to be confident in Him. He doesn't want us to live a life of ease, but rather a life with Him. If He suffered and went through ridicule and scorn for us, what makes us think we won't sometimes suffer the same?

Jesus was willing to put Himself in the lowest position to win us back to Himself. He humbled Himself and put Himself in an uncomfortable position so the Father's mission could be accomplished. What makes us think that as sons and daughters of our Father we will have it any different?

We may not always understand our circumstances or understand the whys. Sometime there won't be any whys. God is willing to put us as bearers of light into dark places, into uncomfortable circumstances, so His mission can be accomplished. Part of our job that our Father asks of us is to lean on Him and trust His leadership.

If we remain confident in Him, and trust our Father's leadership despite our confusion, He can use us as ambassadors of light. He has a purpose in mind. It may not look like what we had in mind, but our job is to keep our eyes on the prize and walk confidently as a son or daughter.

If you suffer for nothing other than living as a Christ follower, then I have good news for you. It means the world sees the One they were hostile to inside of you also! So good job! Keep loving, serving, and practicing your older Brothers example by walking full of grace and truth.

Take some time to make a commitment to model your actions, words, and thoughts after the example left by Jesus. It's far better to suffer for doing what is right than for doing wrong. None of us are perfectly there, so our prayer should be that our Father will show us how to be more like Him.

Notes:

_____

_____

_____

_____

_____

"So Asa went out against him, and they set the troops in battle array in the Valley of Zephathah at Mareshah. And Asa cried out to the Lord God, and said, 'Lord, it is nothing for You to help, whether with many or with those who have no power; help us, O Lord our God, for we rest on You, and in Your name we go against this multitude. O Lord, You are our God; do not let man prevail against You!'"

— 2 Chronicles 14:10-11, NKJV

When the odds are against you, what do you put your rest in? Some put it in themselves and can't rest until they take care of the situation. Some in leaders, spouses, or in having the right job. But even if one of those are your confidence, do you truly rest knowing they will never fail?

What would it look like for you to put your rest in your Father? To rely on Him so much that you believe whatever happens to you happens to Him. That He can help you even if you are powerless to help yourself. And that He can do the impossible.

King Asa built his rest and his confidence on God's promises. He believed that God would take care of His people as they followed and put their trust in their God. That can be easier to do when life is good, but not so much when facing battle lines of armed enemies.

Your Father doesn't rely on what you can do but on what He can do. He can go into the darkest areas of our lives, put His finger on it, and light it up. He can stand before the greatest obstacles, speak a word, and watch it obey Him. He can get close to the hardest of hearts and watch their fear, anger, and doubt melt away.

Nothing is impossible for your Father. But sometimes our hearts betray unbelief when we aren't at rest. And if we aren't at rest, we need to go back to the question: what have we been fostering in our minds and hearts? We must nurture the truth over and over in our heart until we believe it, even if we don't see it.

It is nothing for your Father to do the impossible. Walking through life with a level of expectation that believes this truth is an exciting way to live! It's better to be expectant of good than to be anxious of the potential negatives that might come our way.

———————

Take some time to remind yourself of the promises of your Father. Then take an inventory of all the good He has already brought and all the ways He has kept harm from you. The deeper you search the more the list of good seems endless. Because our Father is the God of endless mercies that always start over fresh each morning.

Notes:

_____

_____

_____

_____

_____

"Jesus answered and said to them, 'Go and tell John the things which you hear and see. The blind see and the lame walk; the lepers are cleansed and the deaf hear; the dead are raised up and the poor have the gospel preached to them. And blessed is he who is not offended because of Me.'"

— Matthew 11:4-6, NKJV

Would you be offended by Jesus? Don't answer right away. All the good Jesus went around doing makes it hard to imagine anyone could be offended by Him. Who could be offended by someone doing so many good works?

But when you see someone receive a blessing while you go without, are you stirred to jealousy? When you see someone else healed, but you still await your day, do you feel set aside? When you feel God speak a hard word that is difficult for you to receive, does pride begin to bristle? Do you feel offended?

Jesus knew when to bring the truth from a heart of love and when to show mercy from a heart of love. Let's not pretend we are any different from those Jesus met. If Jesus walked by you, He would see through you to your heart. And if He called you out and spoke the truth about where you were at, would it cause pride to swell up out of embarrassment? Instead of producing repentance and change, would corrective words stir up anger and resentment in you?

We all hope we would be humble enough to receive what He would say to us. Because the doorway to come to Jesus is repentance and humility. Without it, we hold onto what we have, and are then unable to accept what He has.

Defensiveness can keep us from change, even when we know it is change we need. If Jesus were to confront you about something, what would it be? And if you were called out on it, would you receive it with a heart willing to change?

Instead of letting this question rack you with guilt, use it as a catalyst for growth. Instead of replaying your inadequacies, be purposeful in your pursuit of wholeness in Him. It will take humbling yourself to get there. It will take repentance, and a heart willing to change.

Ask your Father to show you those areas you need to grow in for this season. He may not show it to you the way you want Him to. It may be embarrassing to admit. But God is full of grace and truth, and the chains you may feel now cannot compare to the freedom on the other side.

Notes:

_____

_____

_____

_____

_____

"Look at my Servant, whom I have chosen. He is my Beloved, who pleases me. I will put my Spirit upon him, and he will proclaim justice to the nations. He will not fight or shout or raise his voice in public. He will not crush the weakest reed or put out a flickering candle. Finally he will cause justice to be victorious. And his name will be the hope of all the world."

— Matthew 12:18-21, NLT

Have you ever wondered why God doesn't bring justice right away? Or set all wrong things right when we want Him to. Many even ask the old question: If God is perfect, loving, and just, then why is the world so imperfect, hateful, and unjust? It is a fair question; many genuinely want to know. And our Father isn't afraid of tough questions.

We may not always be able to make sense of the actions of others, other than they are the actions of fallen people in a fallen world. And sometimes in God's mercy we see His intervention in some circumstances. But the answer to the question is the reason people can still be made right with God today.

Jesus is holding back judgement to give you and I time to come to Him before it is too late. How incredibly patient He is! Knowing we will sin, rebel, and totally mess up our lives at times and yet He is willing to walk through the journey with us.

We may be tempted to use this knowledge of the patience of God as a license not to grow or do what's right. But if we do, there will be a day we are confronted. And if God mercifully convicts you, I pray you use it as a catalyst to grow once more.

Once saved, our heart's intent should be to grow. But if our lack of growth means we allow ourselves to live a life of compromise and ignore the conviction of the Spirit, then we are in rebellion against our Father and need to change.

We often fail to realize that if total justice were brought all at once without the wait, even the deep areas of our hearts would have to be dragged out and tried before a just Judge. But there will come a day when Jesus comes again to bring justice on Earth. He will come back to rule over Earth. And those who faithfully did His will while He was away will serve directly with Him when He returns.

Take some time to express your thankfulness to your Father for His patience in bringing justice. It allowed you and I the opportunity to come and be saved. But also, think about what people or situations in your life you can pray over. Pray for His mercy and intervention. We don't know what time we have left, but we can be thankful because His patience is one of the ways He shows us His love.

Notes:

_____

_____

_____

_____

_____

"Then God said to Solomon: 'Because this was in your heart, and you have not asked riches or wealth or honor or the life of your enemies, nor have you asked for long life – but have asked wisdom and knowledge for yourself, that you may judge My people over whom I have made you king – wisdom and knowledge are granted to you; and I will give you riches and wealth and honor, such as none of the kings have had who were before you, nor shall any after you have the like.'"

– 2 Chronicles 1:11-12, NKJV

Solomon had just become king over Israel, and one of the first things he did was go before God to honor Him by sacrificing and seeking His guidance. When God told him to ask of Him, Solomon already had in his heart a longing for wisdom.

Maybe he was intimidated by the prospect of leading a nation. Maybe it had something to do with his father David instilling in him a love for wisdom and seeking after God. But God granted his request and used the gift that He gave to Solomon to bring him everything else he could have asked for.

So it is with the gifts God has planted in you. They are seeds waiting to sprout to life to provide provision, protection, and life to those around you. They are tools given to you by your Father to bring restoration. They can even make room for you when you use them for Him.

When you use your gifts with the wisdom that only comes from above it can be a source of blessing and peace that God can use to change lives.

How are you using and exercising your gifts? Are you around a healthy community of believers that can help sharpen your use of them? Or maybe you don't yet know what God has hidden inside of you for you to discover.

God gave you abilities and gifts for you to be a blessing, both in your family and community. But it can be hard to sharpen your gifting outside your family and community. We all need quality people who can walk in humility with us as we learn and grow. Take your time as you plant yourself so your roots grow down in a good community.

———————

Take some time to do an inventory of the giftings God has given you. How can you sharpen and hone your gifts to be used to serve others? How can you use your gifts to bring financial blessing and healing into your family? And most importantly, are you allowing yourself to be around other believers who can help you in this discovery?

Notes:

_____

_____

_____

_____

_____

"For Ezra had prepared his heart to seek the Law of the LORD, and to do it, and to teach statutes and ordinances in Israel."

— Ezra 7:10, NKJV

Have you prepared your heart to seek God? Not only the act of serving Him, but the preparation and foundation needed for our hearts to be in the right place to serve Him. It would be strange to approach someone I don't know and be completely transparent with them and expect them to reciprocate. Because groundwork is needed to build a relationship for deeper conversations to become normal.

Ezra faced an immense amount of work. Israel had lived for generations in a foreign land and had a lot of learning, and unlearning, to do when God brought them back to their land. And a large part of that responsibility fell on Ezra's shoulders. But he was ready. He had spent the countless hours of preparation in the unseen place and, brick by brick, had allowed God to purpose build him for this task.

So how do we allow our Father to purpose build us? God always wants us to come as we are. But the principle here is God desires us to grow. And what are the requirements for growth in Him? Time with your Father, and lots of it. Surrender, obedience to His ways, commitment, and loyalty are also on the list.

When we have laid the groundwork of time invested as a son or daughter, we can approach our Father knowing His heart and mind. A loyalty that doesn't hold anything against Him, but an openness and honesty that doesn't hide anything from Him either. We all start in a novice state, but God loves us too much to leave us there. He wants to equip us for His purpose.

He is always reaching out, arms extended, giving you and I free choice to grow or not to grow closer to Him. He won't force your growth or force you to be near Him. He wants you to want to. God is super generous though, and oftentimes when we take a step towards Him, He takes several towards us.

So, how close do you want to be with your Father?

———

Take some time and think over the implications of this question. After careful thought, give your genuine answer. What steps are you willing to take to spend time with Him? Give Him your honest answers, then listen for His voice so you can begin the growth.

Notes:

_____

_____

_____

_____

_____

"But without faith it is impossible to please Him, for he who comes to God must believe that He is, and that He is a rewarder of those who diligently seek Him."

— Hebrews 11:6, NKJV

"But Jesus said, 'Let the children come to me. Don't stop them! For the Kingdom of Heaven belongs to those who are like these children.'"

— Matthew 19:14, NLT

Have you ever had a workout buddy or personal trainer who always pushed you for *just one more*? And then, after that, did they push you for just one more again and again until you truly reached your limit?

If we give up on anything, we may never see the results of what could have been. Sometimes that breakthrough comes only through persistence. We see this in our personal times with our Father also. "Just one more minute with You, Father. Can I worship you a little longer? I love to hear Your voice, can you speak to me again one more time? One more worship song, oh please, oh please?" How would our devotional time change if we pursued Him like this?

This kind of childlike persistence motivated by love drives the Father to respond. He is drawn to it. What father wouldn't be? What would be the result if we also chose *just once more* in other areas? Like honoring, loving, and respecting our spouse? Or *just once more* to being patient and gentle with our kids? Or giving our all at our work?

If we act in our own effort and strength, even the strongest will eventually tap out. We all have natural limits and need to be trained and tested to go further than before. And your Father, just like that personal trainer, is right beside you saying: "Just once more!" Only this time, instead of striving, you can do it through His strength. One more time you can show love to your neighbor. One more time you can show up for those who need someone. One more time you can pray for someone. One more time you can choose to carry peace.

We often forget that our Father loves to gives *just one more* also. When we fail, He stands ready to forgive one more time if we are ready to come back to Him. Once more, and even a thousand once more's He leads patiently. He cheers each wobbly step forward. And instead of kicking us to the curb, He patiently brings loving correction to bring us back to Him.

———————

Take some time to look at areas in your life that need persistence. Ask God to give you His strength and peace as you walk into those areas. And when you are tempted to give up, set your eyes on your Father and hear Him say to you: "Just one more!"

Notes:

_____

_____

_____

_____

"As you therefore have received Christ Jesus the Lord, so walk in Him, rooted and built up in Him and established in the faith, as you have been taught, abounding in it with thanksgiving."

– Colossians 2:6-7, NKJV

We all know how tall and majestic a tree looks, rising high into the sky. But you wouldn't be able to see the beauty of the tree above without the unseen growth below. It's the messiness of the roots that beautifies the leaves. It's the sturdy anchor of the deep roots that allows the tree to sway gently without fear. It's the appetite of the roots that draws life from deep waters to feed the tree. And as the tree grows, what falls from its branches supply life to other plants that are nearby.

Just like trees, it is our time with our Father in the secret place that feeds our spirit and gives us life. This time enables us to operate as our Father intended. For our spirit to grow we must put our roots down deep in our Father and His Word. This hidden time of worshiping and praying, of listening, and of opening ourselves completely to our Father enables us to walk confidently in public as a son or daughter of Him.

But before we can grow *up,* we must first grow *down* by planting ourselves firmly in our Father and His promises.

No tree is promised good weather all the time. But if you anchor yourself deeply you can weather the storms you will face. And if those storms cause you to bear scars, those scars will be a sign of your Fathers faithfulness to see you through.

Your Father allows some storms to come as an opportunity to drive your roots deeper with Him and in His Word. But the choice is always ours. We can choose to grow or not to. And if we choose to ground ourselves in Him, we can grow tall, confident not in our own ability but in our Father to weather us through.

Take some time to study your roots. Have you grown *down* with your Father? Have you made enough time to build a foundation with Him? The choice is always ours to make. Your Father will not force you, but like any good parent He desperately wants that time with you. He sees your potential and wants you to reach it more than you do. But first comes the downward growth. The door is open. Will you walk through?

Notes:

_____

_____

_____

_____

_____

"And Mordecai told them to answer Esther: 'Do not think in your heart that you will escape in the kings palace any more than all the other Jews. For if you remain completely silent at this time, relief and deliverance will arise for the Jews from another place, but you and your father's house will perish. Yet who knows whether you have come to the kingdom for such a time as this?'"

— Esther 4:13-14, NKJV

Have you ever felt that your actions don't matter? That if you don't act someone else will, so why bother? Someone else is probably more qualified and can do it better anyway, right?

In Esther we see the plot of Haman to kill all Jews in the Babylonian Empire on one set day. God had already said He wouldn't let His people be destroyed, and I'm sure Mordecai believed this also. God wouldn't let that take place; He would defend His people. But if Easter chose not to act, how many would have died before God used someone else?

The problem with thinking what we do doesn't matter is that it destroys possibilities. It rips away the opportunity for those around you. You can go along not acting, and God will have His ultimate will in the earth. But what will be the condition of those directly around us if we choose not to act?

Just like the question of how many plants are in a seed can't be answered, so one action or word can birth more possibilities into endless possibilities based on one obedience. One action, one word, one prayer, one obedience at a time creates ripples far from our own sphere of influence.

Who wants to watch sports games where players have the attitude that their actions don't matter? Who wants to give to charities who have this mentality? Our every action makes a difference for the future. But the only way to see it is to sow it in faith. Later in life, when you are surrounded by answered prayers and the fruits of the actions you chose, will you believe it to be worth it then?

Take some time and examine yourself for any areas in which you need to act. Ask God to reveal any other areas you might not see yet. If you are uncertain of how, ask God for wisdom in handling the situation. There is a lot of safety in getting good counsel (Proverbs 11:14). Do everything out of a heart of love, and when it is your turn to do the right thing, bravely choose to act.

Notes:

_____

_____

_____

_____

_____

"Show me Your ways, O Lord; Teach me Your paths."

— Psalm 25:4, NKJV

*"The secret things belong to the Lord our God, but those
things which are revealed belong to us and to our children
forever, that we may do all the words of this law."*

— Deuteronomy 29:29, NKJV

Do you want to know your Father's secrets? Do you wish He would explain what He is doing? The position of *not knowing* can be a difficult place to be in, especially for those who don't like feeling out of control.

His secrets belong to Him. They are gifts that can be given to friends who choose to be close (John 15:15). God doesn't keep secrets from you to harm you. God loves sharing His secrets because, like in an Easter egg hunt, He has hidden mysteries and secrets for you. He loves it when your face lights up as you discover something new. But we must first search in the right places.

The depth of God's knowledge and the complexity of His creation are so immense we could spend eternity watching Him slowly peel back and reveal each layer for us, like the layers of an onion. And He wants to share those secrets with His friends.

But a friend only shares secrets with other friends. And conversations only grow deeper the more time you spend with someone. This requires an investment of your time. Time in the secret place, and walking with Him in public. Keeping your mind and heart in the same place as His as you go about your day. When you do, you won't just know about Him, you'll know His ways and how He operates.

What we value we will put time into. And what we don't value we will withhold time from. It is such a simple test of where our heart is in every area of our life. It doesn't lie, either.

Like a child who can't wait to share their secrets with their friends, so God loves to reveal His secrets with those who want to get closer to Him. And this opportunity is accessible for all to take advantage of. The least to the greatest all get an equal number of hours in a day. Hours given to us by God. Like a good Father, He gives us the time and then steps back to see how we will use it. But no one knows how many days we have, so make each one count!

———

Take some time to evaluate where your time has been going to. If too much time is being spent on things that don't matter, then restructure your time and invest it more into those things that do matter. Time spent with your Father, your family, serving, and in growth towards your calling is always time well spent.

Notes:

_____

_____

_____

_____

"I know your works, your labor, your patience, and that you cannot bear those who are evil. And you have tested those who say they are apostles and are not, and have found them liars; and you have persevered and have patience, and have labored for My name's sake and have not become weary. Nevertheless I have this against you, that you have left your first love. Remember therefore from where you have fallen; repent and do the first works…"

— Revelation 2:2-5a, NKJV

Do you ever feel you don't have the same love you once had towards Jesus?

Love makes us do strange things. Things like showing kindness and mercy to those who hate us. Things like forgiving others who hurt us. Even humbling ourselves and elevating others. These are kingdom actions and flow from the heart of God!

But what would happen if you wanted to do the right thing but didn't *feel the love* anymore, and your close times with Him were fewer and fewer? You would probably have to work hard, strive, and go through the motions. You would have to push yourself and fake feelings of caring. And instead of acting from the law of love, which comes from a heart changed by the love of God, you'd have to act from a list of laws, rules, and principles.

We must have good laws and rules. And a principled life is admirable. But the problem is the forgotten source. It is so like Jesus to skip over everything we see as success and go straight to the heart! Notice He commends their works, then calls them out for lack of love, and then says to do works. But not just any works, their first works.

All the works they were doing were good, but how do you behave when you are in love?

A marriage relationship can go through the motions for a long time with both sides working hard. But how gut-wrenching it would be for your spouse to say to you: "you don't love me anymore." The works were all there, but the works that stem from a heart of love were not.

Our love for God is best manifested in our obedience to Him. And one of the most important commands from Jesus was to love others. So important that God said if we don't love others, we don't love Him (1 John 4). And if you find your heart colder than it used to be, then it is time for your *first love* to have first place once again.

―――――――――

If you feel a lack of love towards Jesus, your brothers and sisters in Christ, or others around you, take some time to get back into the secret place in repentance. First ask God what areas of your heart are out of sync with His heart. Repent for those things and ask God to begin changing your heart. Our part then is to begin showing unconditional love. Unconditional love that first flowed from the heart of our Father.

Notes:

_____

_____

_____

_____

_____

"Then the Lord said to Moses, 'Make a fiery serpent, and set it on a pole; and it shall be that everyone who is bitten, when he looks at it, shall live.'"

— Numbers 21:8, NKJV

"He removed the high places and broke the sacred pillars, cut down the wooden image and broke in pieces the bronze serpent that Moses had made; for until those days the children of Israel burned incense to it, and called it Nehushtan."

— 2 Kings 18:4, NKJV

Beware trusting in the supply rather than the Supplier. Beware becoming captivated with what is provided rather than your Source. Beware letting your blessing steal your focus instead of fixing your gaze on the Giver of all good gifts.

Israel created a problem and God created a solution. That solution was God's way of turning Israel's focus back to Him as their one true God. Many years later, what God had used to draw His people back to Him was now being used to draw Israel away. The solution had turned into a problem because they focused more on the supply, than on the Supplier. When they did, that supply was rightly broken up so Israel would look to nothing but God.

God's solutions are meant to bring us back to Him, not to take His place. Can you imagine giving your child a gift that brings them joy, and then after a while, they want nothing to do with you but only want the thing you gave them? Would it stir a healthy jealousy in you as a father or mother? Because we want what we give our children to bring them closer to us as a family.

The serpent on a pole was symbolic of God's plan to save all who would turn from the poisonous bite of the first serpent and look to the One who was sent to take all that poison on Himself. The wood of the cross is long gone, but our living hope Jesus is alive! Our attention must be drawn to the One who died to make a way for us back to the Father.

Take some time to evaluate if any good things brought into your life have now become a distraction. Has anything crossed the line from being a provided blessing to becoming an idol? Is there anything that takes your focus, energy, or time away from your one true Source? If there is, call it out, repent of it, release it, break it up, and turn your focus back to your Father.

Notes:

_____

_____

_____

_____

_____

"Therefore we also, since we are surrounded by so great a cloud of witnesses, let us lay aside every weight, and the sin which so easily ensnares us, and let us run with endurance the race that is set before us."

— Hebrews 12:1, NKJV

A hiker that remains at home may stay safe and comforted. At least until their bodies slowly waste away and can no longer make the journey. But those who are willing to set foot on the trail will encounter more adventure and beauty than those who chose to stay comforted. Are we willing to take that risk, that leap, and follow our Father when He walks into places unknown?

Sometimes, our problem is that we have too many things that weigh us down. It may be secret sins, wounds we haven't let heal, doubts, fears. It may also be that we, deep down, don't really trust our Father.

Any hiker knows that the heavier your pack, the slower and more worn out you will be. So why do we carry so much? Possibly because the longer we carry something the more we feel like it is ours to carry.

Bitterness and unforgiveness are heavier than sand. Anxiety and worry are like a sack of rocks. Fear and doubt add bricks to our packs. So why do we carry them? Is it because we want to? Or that we don't know yet how to fully lay them down?

But Jesus, just like the best hiking companion, offers to trade our heavy pack for His perfectly fitted, lighter pack. He is strong enough and wants you to run free with Him. We need endurance to run the race of life and carrying a heavy pack just won't do.

So how do we do it? First, find someone trustworthy to take the walk with you. Don't hike alone in this. Be intentional and name what it is that is keeping you locked up. Then take it to God and release it to Him. Say, "God this is yours now, I want what You have for what I have." Then trade it, and don't pick it back up.

This can sometimes be a long process and may require going through steps. Bitterness, hurt, and unforgiveness are all chains that need to be broken. It may have taken you a long time to get off course, but that doesn't always mean it will take as long to get back on the trail. God can redeem the time.

Take some time to pinpoint what might be hindering full freedom in your life with your Father. What are you carrying in your pack that you shouldn't? Take whatever that *thing* is and agree to the most unfair trade of all time: our worst for God's best.

Notes:

_____

_____

_____

_____

_____

"You shall not take the name of the Lord your God in vain, for the Lord will not hold him guiltless who takes His name in vain."

– Exodus 20:7, NKJV

Have you ever done something lightly, not thinking it through? Many of us have, sometimes only to regret it later. Or have you spoken lightly or disrespectfully of another person?

The common understanding of the 3rd commandment is to not use God's name as profanity. Although I agree, this partial interpretation seems odd since the other commandments seem far weightier. Like two people reading vows to each other, promising fidelity from that moment onward.

On the mountain of Sinai, God was beginning a covenant with Israel, much like a wedding ceremony. First were promises to have no one else before Him, to love Him with everything inside them. Then a charge to Israel to not take His name, or the covenant they were entering, lightly. But instead, many of them did not take it seriously and soon after cheated and had affairs with other gods.

What was our view of God when we were first saved? Do we think God's name is empty and hollow, or do we believe miracles can happen when we use the name of Jesus? Do we use *Christian* as our title to exalt ourselves over others, or hold His name as a gift and an honor to carry inside our *earthen vessel*? Do we speak the name of God as if He were a mythical figure, or as the High King sworn to come again to reign over the earth?

We all have failed our Father at times. If not for God's forgiveness, we would all be guilty of dishonoring and holding lightly God's name and the covenant we made with Him. And if you don't feel you have His forgiveness in this area, you are in luck. Because if you ask for it, you can receive it today!

Take some time to reflect on your covenant with Christ. Have you been holding your relationship with Him with fidelity of heart? If you have regarded His name as common or taken lightly the salvation bought for you, then repent and start fresh. Your Father always wants you back. But you must be totally His, with all your heart, soul, mind, and strength.

Notes:

_____

_____

_____

_____

"The Lord isn't really being slow about his promise, as some people think. No, he is being patient for your sake. He does not want anyone to be destroyed, but wants everyone to repent."

— 2 Peter 3:9, NLT

"But we all, with unveiled face, beholding as in a mirror the glory of the Lord, are being transformed into the same image from glory to glory, just as by the Spirit of the Lord."

— 2 Corinthians 3:18, NKJV

Have you ever continued in a type of behavior for a while before the Spirit finally convicted you? If so, have you ever wondered why He allowed you to continue for so long before conviction set in?

The absence of God's conviction does not imply the presence of His approval. Like a good parent, our Father set the standards in place long beforehand, making it evident in everything He made (Romans 1:19-20). We have a responsibility to examine our hearts, our motives, and our actions. Not to condemn ourselves, but to use sober judgement based on our Father's words when evaluating our conduct.

Sanctification is both a destination and a journey. It is where divine perfection meets imperfect creation and begins the process of drawing us upward. God understands our failings and is patient with us. He sees our whole timeline and doesn't expect perfection all at once.

But we are not passive observers in this process. When we recognize something in us that does not align with God's heart or Word, we make a choice how to respond. Whether that be through action or inaction.

But how can we be changed into that image without the consistent and constant time in the mirror of His Word? When we read our Father's love letter from heaven, we begin to see more how our hearts and minds should align to be more like His. One area at a time, one issue at a time, one step at a time. Only the hands of the Master Creator could patiently work with us until we are made new each day.

Take some time to examine your heart. Not to beat yourself up, but with an attitude of humility that accepts we all have areas needing growth. Examine your motives and attitudes. Put yourself in a quiet place and allow your Father to gently put His finger on any area He wants to see growth in. He wants you to join Him in the process. And any project He begins with you He will faithfully and patiently finish!

Notes:

_____

_____

_____

_____

_____

"Therefore do not worry about tomorrow, for tomorrow will worry about its own things. Sufficient for the day is its own trouble."

— *Matthew 6:34, NKJV*

Notice Jesus didn't say not to plan for tomorrow. He didn't say not to have goals or organize your future steps. He just said not to worry about it. Plan, organize, set goals, then walk it out with confidence and without worry.

It's so much better to daydream about the good *what-ifs* than to be paralyzed in worry over the bad *what-ifs*.

Why don't we genuinely believe our Father has good plans for us? Instead, we betray a lack of belief in the goodness of God with our inner worry.

Just like a gauge that displays when something is out of alignment, so it is with our beliefs when we walk through life. Your emotions will follow your inner beliefs, eventually falling in line with what we truly believe. If you continually worry you might not have a feelings problem, but an unbelief problem.

We all face challenges, but our Father has good plans for us. The question is, do we really believe in the goodness of our Father to be our provider?

If not, dig into His Word and see what He promised when it comes to provision and faithfulness. Look to see if those promises have conditions that must be met. Once you are armed and washed with the truth, take the time to engage your will to put it into practice.

Take some time to examine your core beliefs about God's faithfulness and provision. Ask yourself the tough questions. God isn't afraid of tough questions, and neither should we. Do you truly believe God will be faithful to what He promised you in His Word? Can you lean on that even if you can't see what is ahead?

Notes:

_____

_____

_____

_____

_____

"Now Jabez was more honorable than his brother, and his mother called his name Jabez, saying, 'Because I bore him in pain.' And Jabez called on the God of Israel saying, 'Oh, that You would bless me indeed, and enlarge my territory, that Your hand would be with me, and that You would keep me from evil, that I may not cause pain!' So God granted him what he requested."

— 1 Chronicles 4:9-10, NKJV

"Until now you have asked nothing in My name. Ask, and you will receive, that your joy may be full."

— John 16:24, NKJV

God likes an open and honest heart. Jabez had words spoken over him, even the meaning of his name, that he carried into his life. Instead of resigning himself to be what others spoke over him, he decided he wanted a course change.

Jabez openly and honestly asked God to bless him so he wouldn't cause others pain or be a financial burden or embarrassment to his family. Instead, he wanted to be a joy and a blessing to those around him. He wanted the curse of his name broken, but he also wanted that curse to become a blessing.

I believe God honored his request in part because of the why. He wasn't asking selfishly, but genuinely didn't want to cause harm or pain to others.

What do you want to ask your Father for? He is merciful and loving, but also just. What is in your heart to be able to bless others with? Ask for it. Ask that your joy may be full. Sometimes we end up surprised that what we had is really all we needed. But at other times, we find out we didn't have something because we never asked for it.

I've wondered before what I would say or do if I could have a few minutes with a world or national leader. Would I ask for something, or would I criticize? Would I bring up a cause I felt passionate about? Or would I clam up when given the rare opportunity to speak to a powerful leader who might be able to do something?

Take some time to remember something simple but powerful. That you, a son or daughter of God because of our big Brother Jesus, can at any time have an audience with the Highest King who CAN do anything. And He's telling you to ask away. What will you ask?

Notes:

_____

_____

_____

_____

_____

"And they were helped against them, and the Hagrites were delivered into their hand, and all who were with them, for they cried out to God in the battle. He heeded their prayer, because they put their trust in Him."

— 1 Chronicles 5:20, NKJV

"The Lord is my strength and my shield; My heart trusted in Him, and I am helped; Therefore my heart greatly rejoices, and with my song I will praise Him."

— Psalm 28:7, NKJV

When the heat gets turned up in your life, what do you turn to? We all reflexively turn to a source in times of stress. Some are better, some are worse. Most do little more than help us cope for a while. But what if you had a source that never failed you?

We all trust in something. What do you trust in? Who do you trust in? The list for most people is very short. Our actions when it comes to trust are far more revealing than our words; that's why trying times reveal more about what we are made of than average times.

Trust is built on a history of experiences and can be grown or lost over time. If you have never extended trust towards your Father, you may have trouble trusting Him at first. David had a long history of extending trust to God and was able to have confidence in Him because God was true to His word.

It's a shame most Christians don't extend trust to God in all the areas He made strong promises in. But like testing a railing before fully leaning on it, how would you learn all those ways if you never tested them?

We may say we trust God with finances, but do we tithe or give to those in need? If you believe prayer can change what is around you, do you commit to serious and continuous prayer on a regular basis? If you believe your Father will supply all your needs, do you choose to continue to give and invest in your spouse and family even when your needs aren't being met?

Some have hurts and wounds due to the actions of others, so trust may not come easy. If this is you, remember God is full of patience and understanding, and will meet you where you are. Bring it back to the basics and start reminding yourself of the promises God gave in His word. Memorize them until they are a part of you. Meditate on them until they flow naturally. Then test them by putting them into practice.

———

Take some time to grow your trust in your Father. What promises has He made in His word that you can begin to lean on? In what areas can your confidence grow in His faithfulness? And if your confidence in an area is low, it is time to begin to test His promises in that area.

Notes:

_____

_____

_____

_____

Printed in the United States
by Baker & Taylor Publisher Services